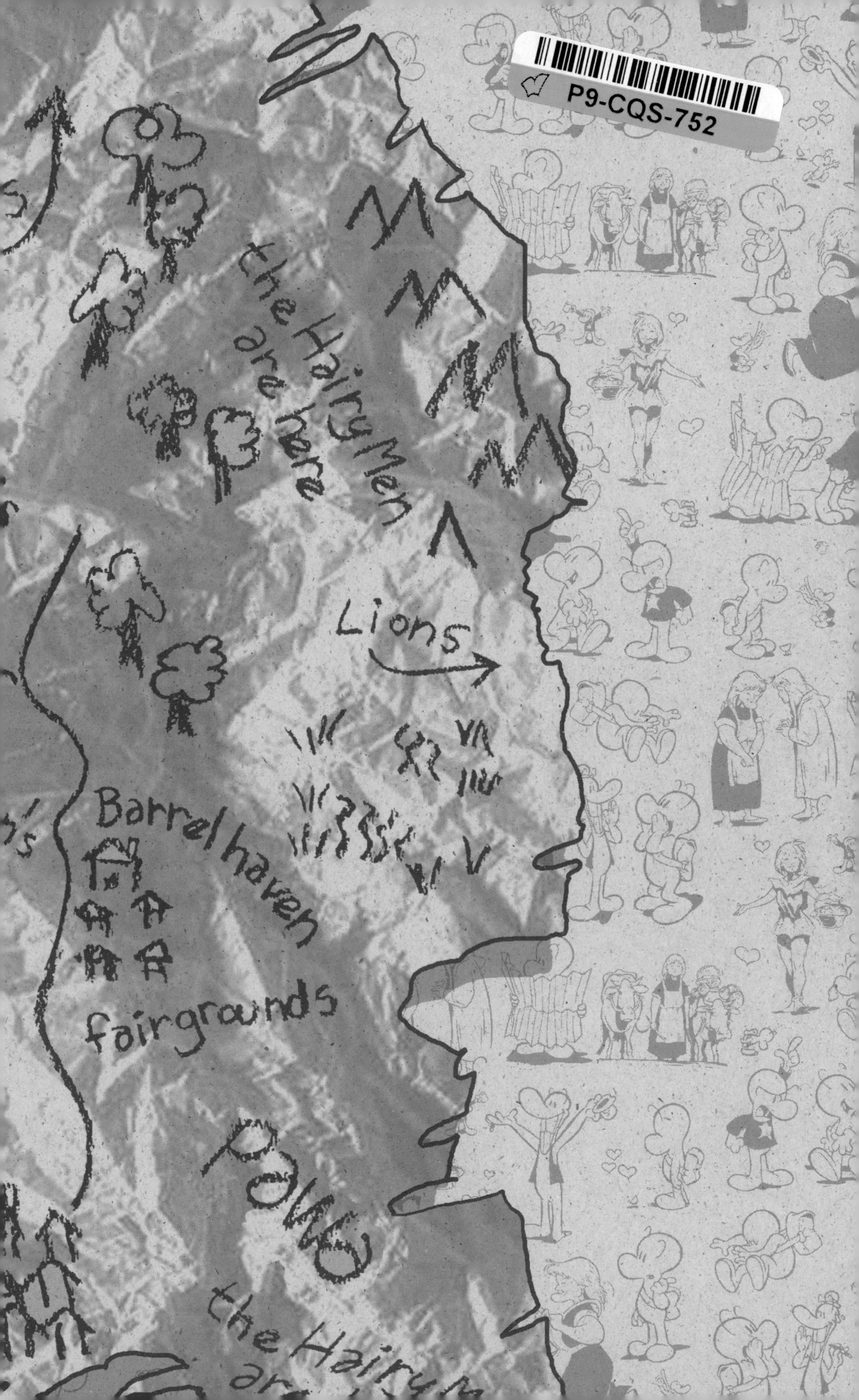
the Hairy Men are here
Lions
Barrelhaven
fairgrounds

Part One

(Vernal Equinox)

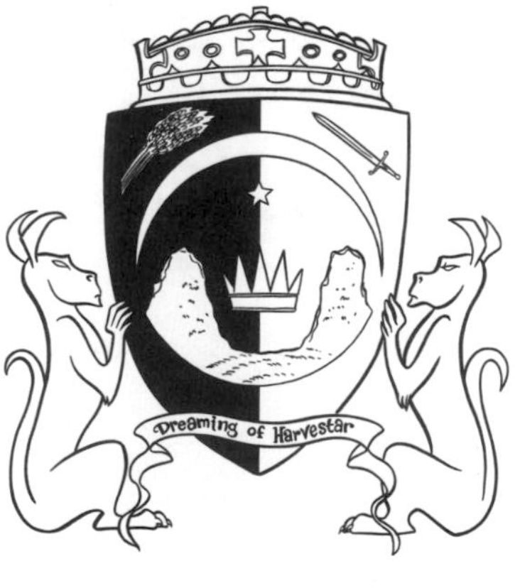
Dreaming of Harvestar

Volume One:
Out From Boneville

Jeff Smith

Cartoon Books
Columbus, Ohio

THIS BOOK IS
FOR
VIJAYA

BONE Volume ONE: Out From Boneville copyright © 1996 by Jeff Smith.

Acknowledgements: The Harvestar Family Crest designed by Charles Vess.
For information write:
Cartoon Books
P.O. Box 16973
Columbus, OH 43216

First Edition

Softcover ISBN: 0-9636609-4-2
Hardcover ISBN: 0-9636609-9-3

Library of Congress Catalog Card Number (hardcover): 95-068403

10 98765432

Printed in Canada

8

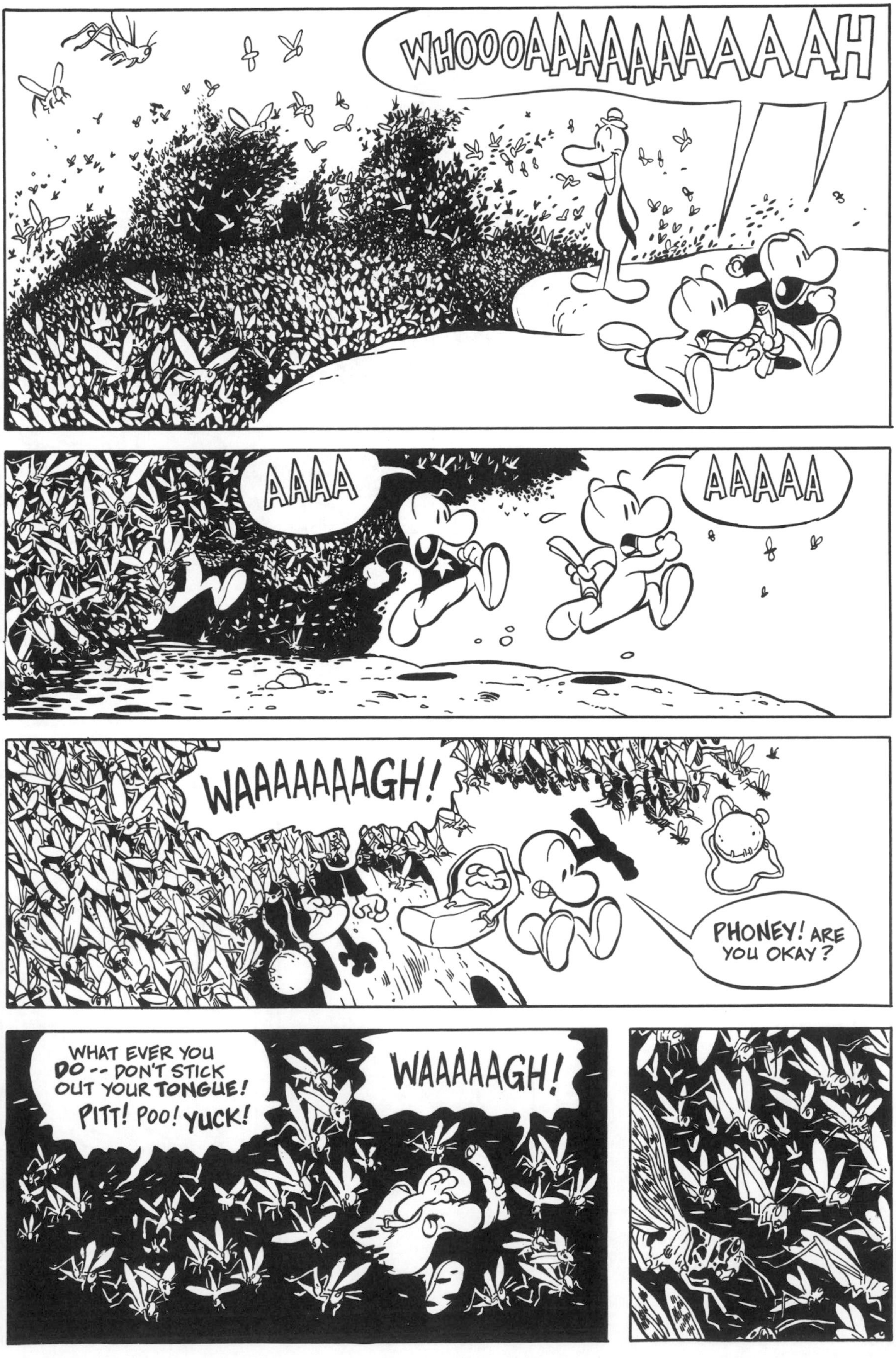
WHOOOAAAAAAAAAAAH
AAAA
AAAAA
WAAAAAAAGH!
PHONEY! ARE YOU OKAY?
WHAT EVER YOU DO -- DON'T STICK OUT YOUR TONGUE! PITT! POO! YUCK!
WAAAAAGH!

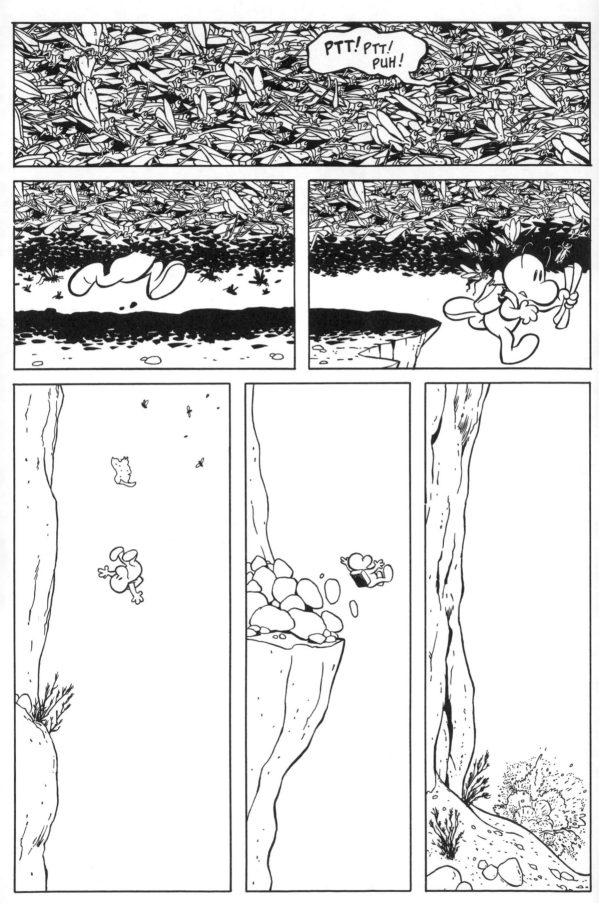

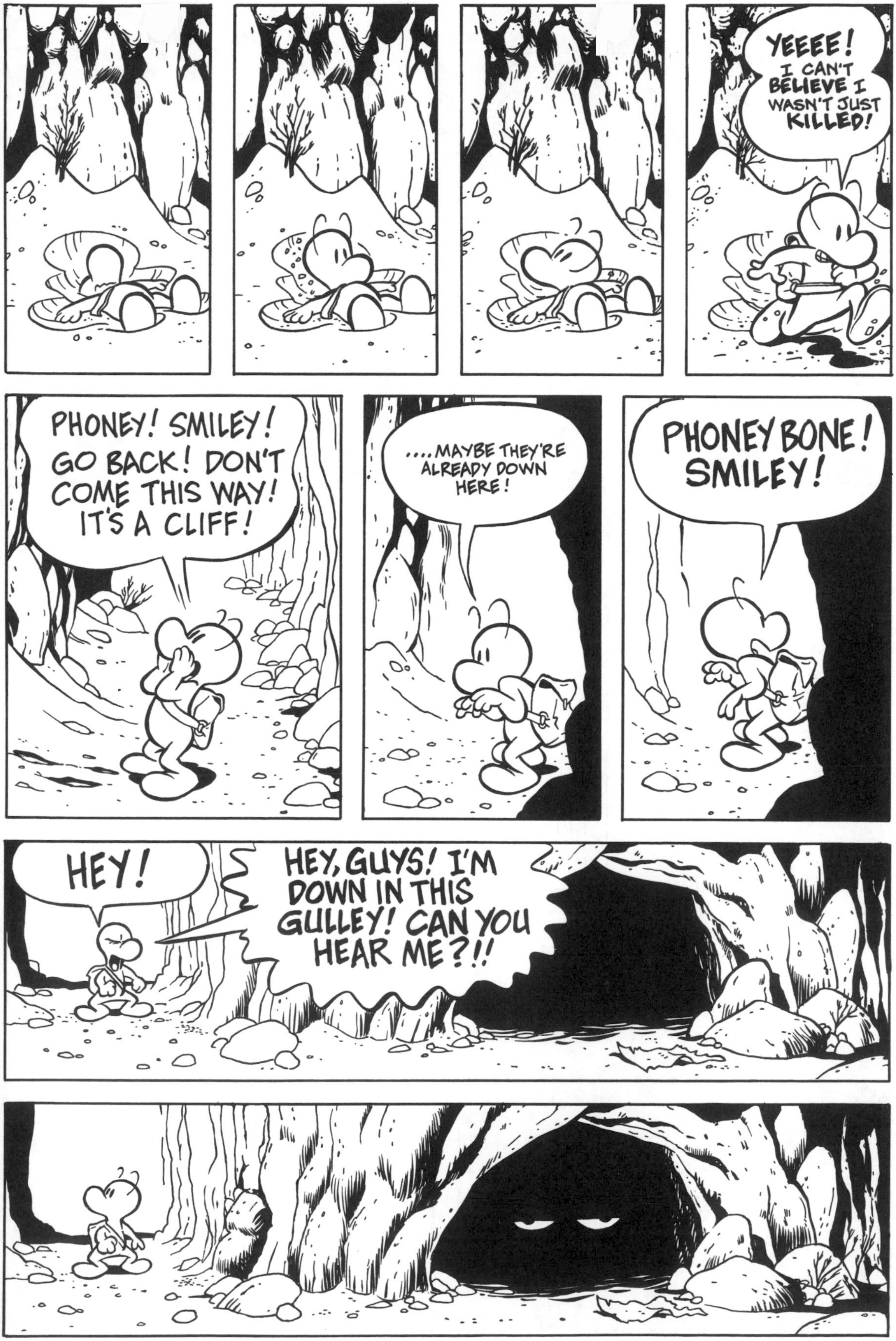
YEEEE! I CAN'T BELIEVE I WASN'T JUST KILLED!
PHONEY! SMILEY! GO BACK! DON'T COME THIS WAY! IT'S A CLIFF!
....MAYBE THEY'RE ALREADY DOWN HERE!
PHONEY BONE! SMILEY!
HEY!
HEY, GUYS! I'M DOWN IN THIS GULLEY! CAN YOU HEAR ME?!!

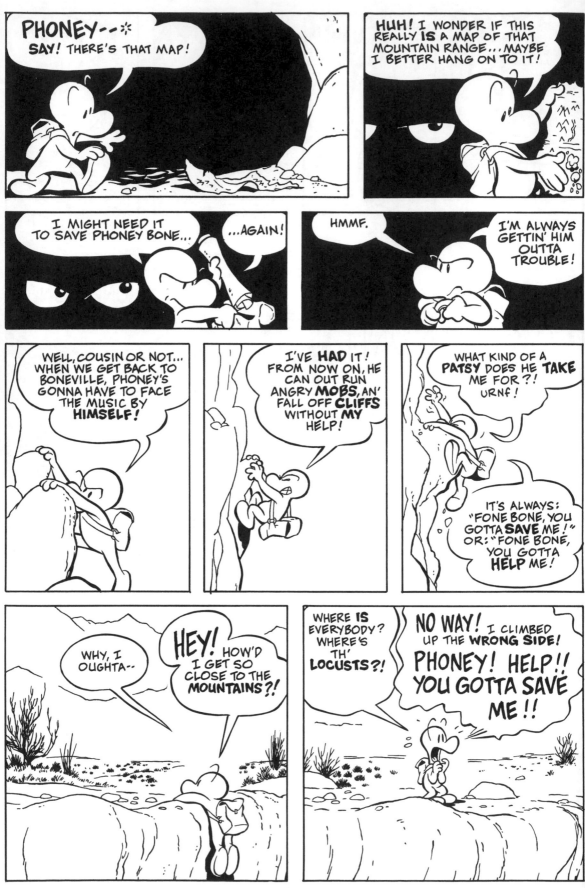

14

15

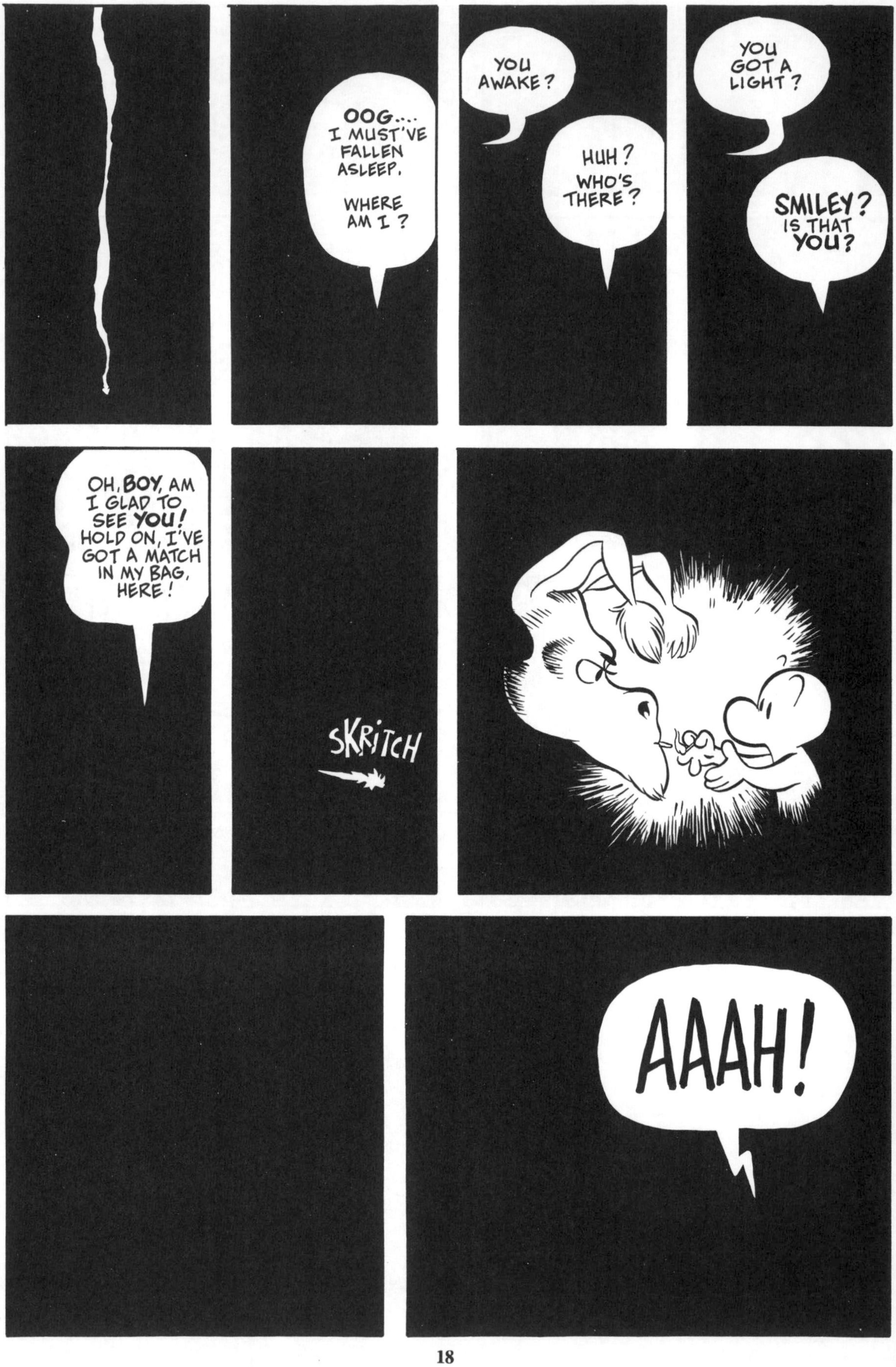
OOG... I MUST'VE FALLEN ASLEEP.
WHERE AM I ?
YOU AWAKE ?
HUH ? WHO'S THERE ?
YOU GOT A LIGHT ?
SMILEY? IS THAT YOU?
OH, BOY, AM I GLAD TO SEE YOU! HOLD ON, I'VE GOT A MATCH IN MY BAG, HERE!
SKRITCH
AAAH!

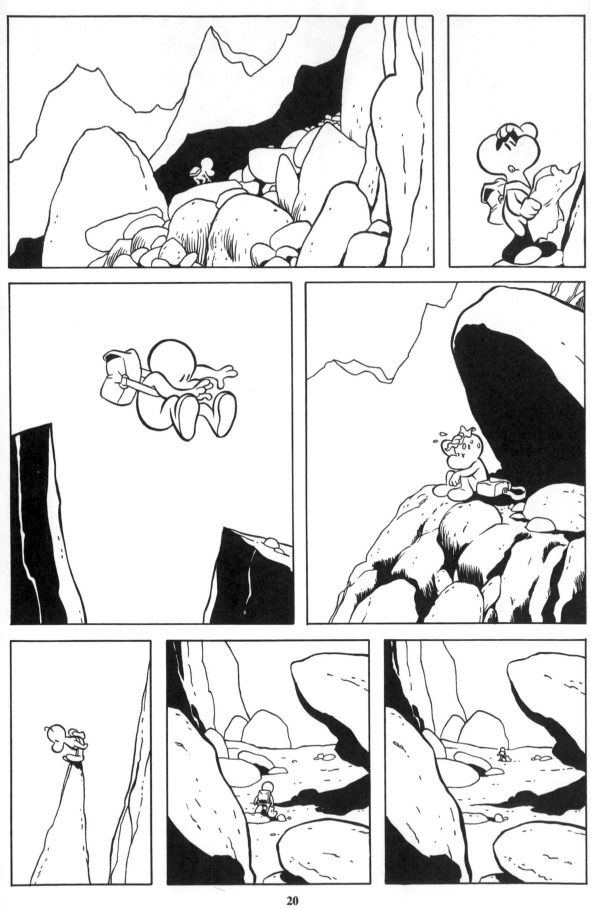

COOL.

I MADE IT!

THAT STUPID MAP WAS **RIGHT!** YESSIREE, **BOB!** THERE'S WATER ON TH' MENU **TONIGHT!**

I COULD **KISS** SMILEY BONE FOR FINDING THAT MAP!

I MIGHT EVEN KISS **PHONEY** RIGHT BEFORE I STRANGLE HIM!

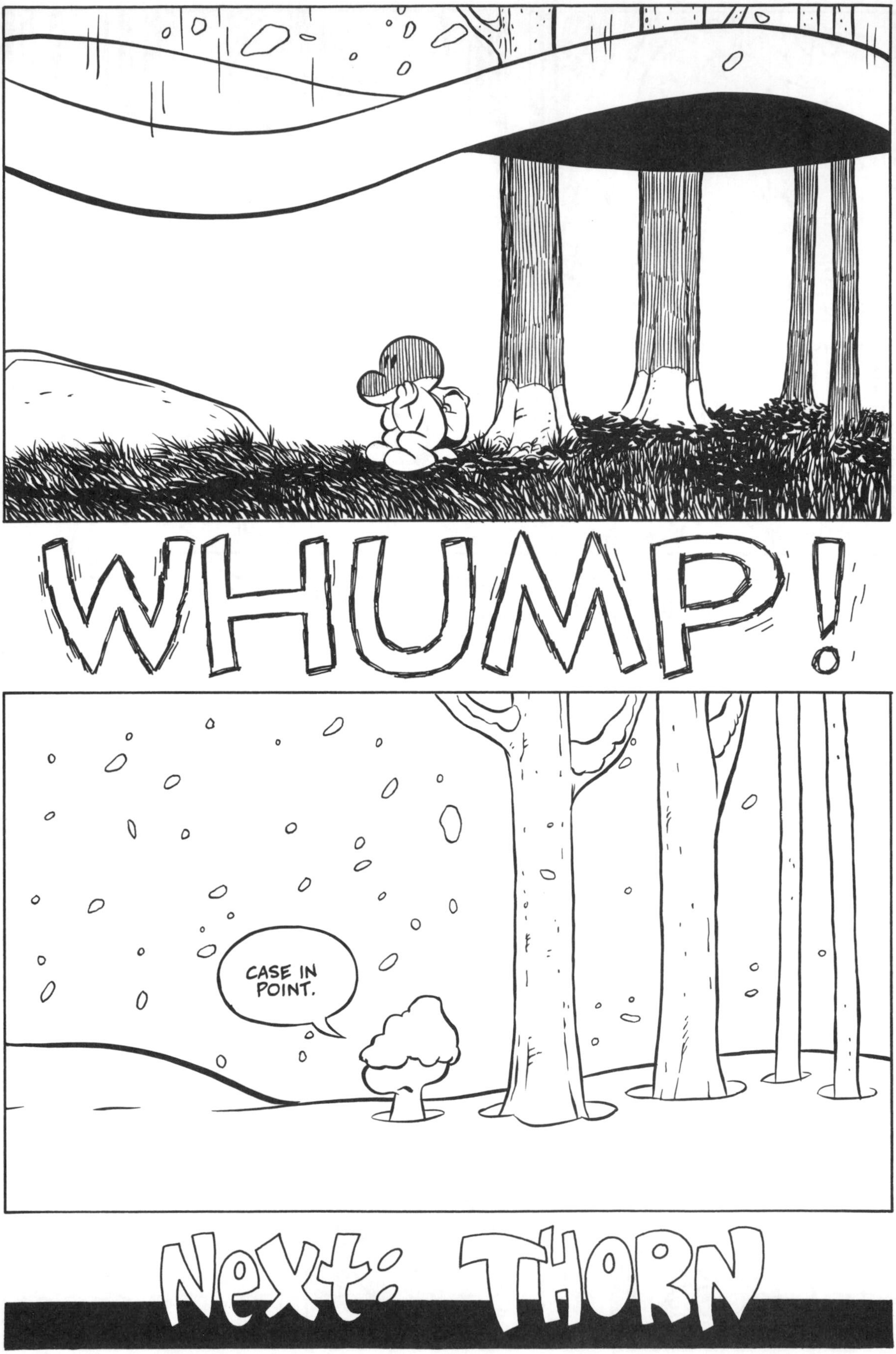
WHUMP!
CASE IN POINT.
Next: THORN

31

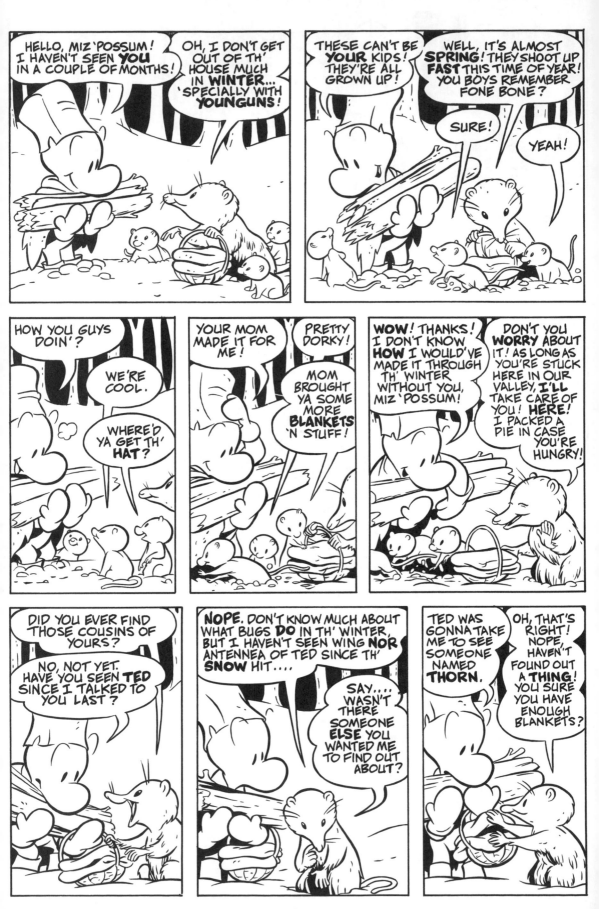

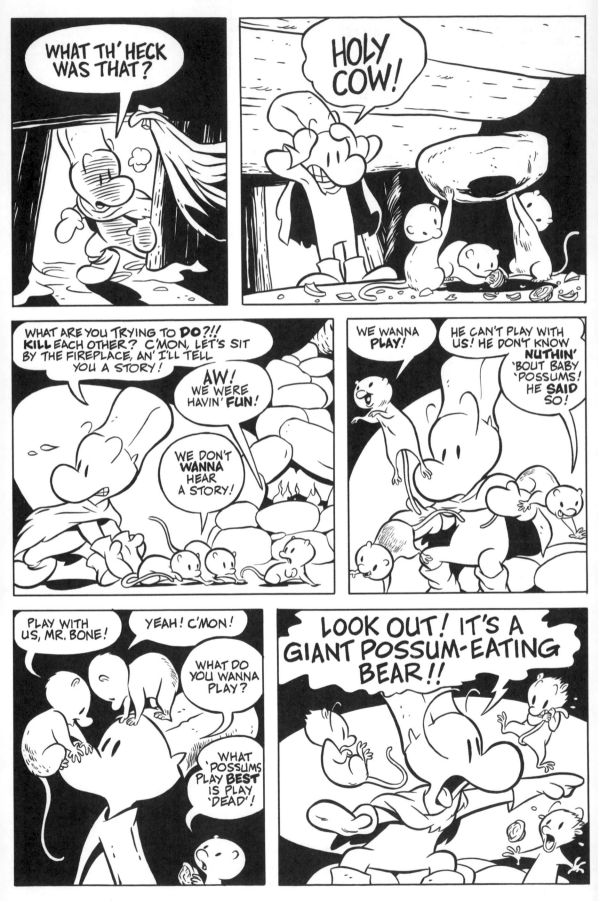

34

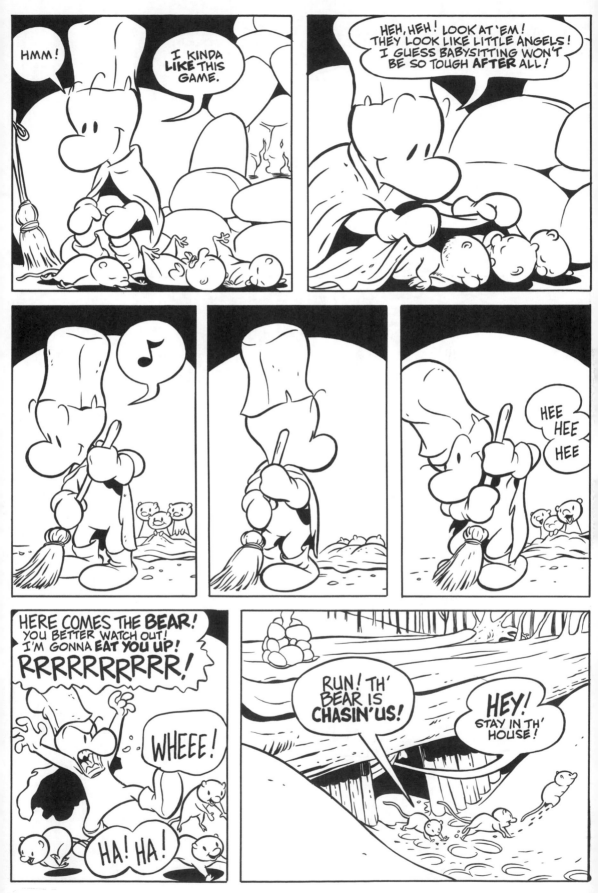

35

36

THOSE RAT CREATURES WOULD HAVE TO BE PRETTY STUPID TO FOLLOW ME ON TO THIS FRAIL, LITTLE BRANCH!

STUPID, STUPID RAT CREATURES!!

42

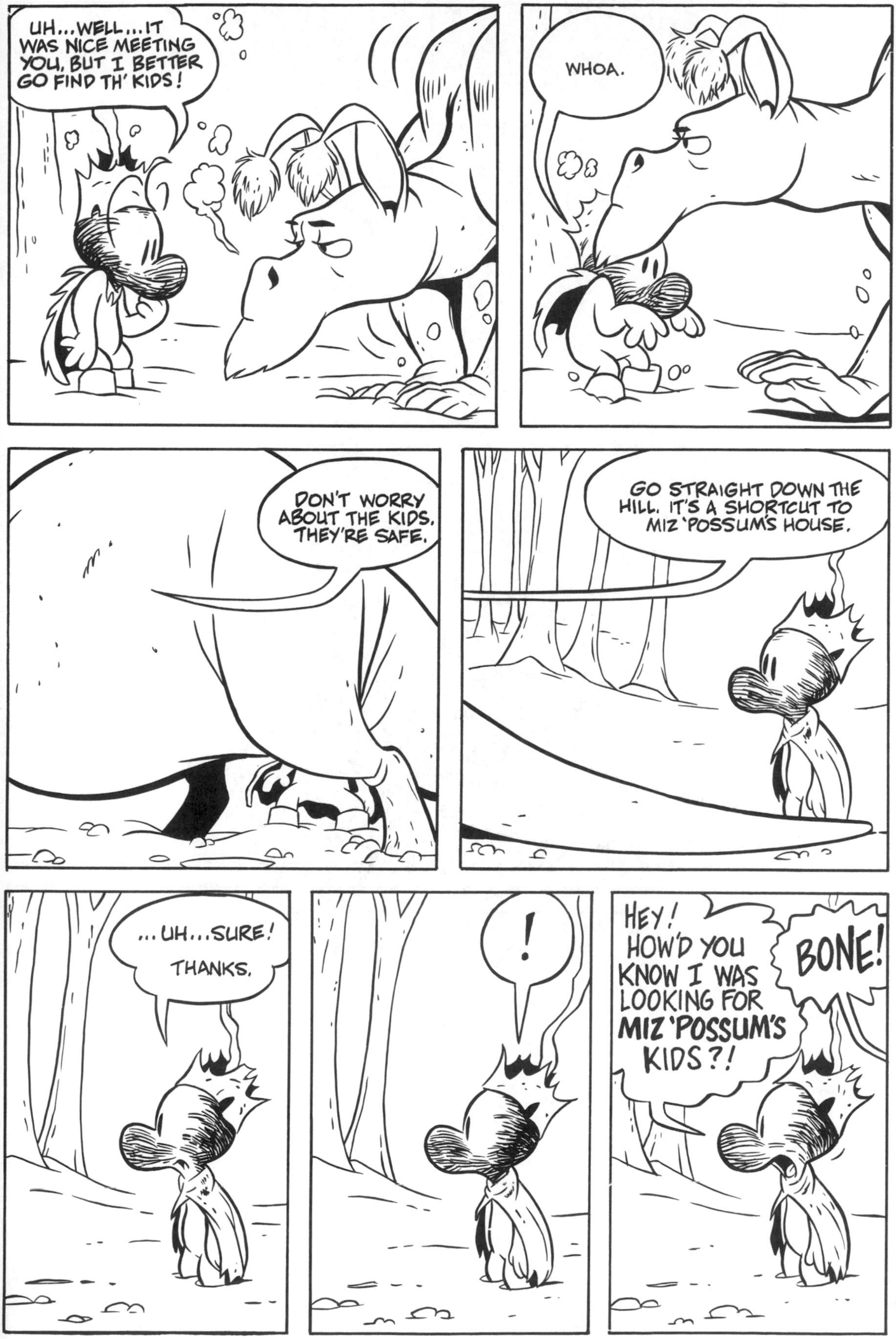
UH...WELL...IT WAS NICE MEETING YOU, BUT I BETTER GO FIND TH' KIDS!
WHOA.
DON'T WORRY ABOUT THE KIDS. THEY'RE SAFE.
GO STRAIGHT DOWN THE HILL. IT'S A SHORTCUT TO MIZ 'POSSUM'S HOUSE.
...UH...SURE! THANKS.
!
HEY! HOW'D YOU KNOW I WAS LOOKING FOR MIZ 'POSSUM'S KIDS?!
BONE!

44

♪ MMMMMM ♪

FOOM!

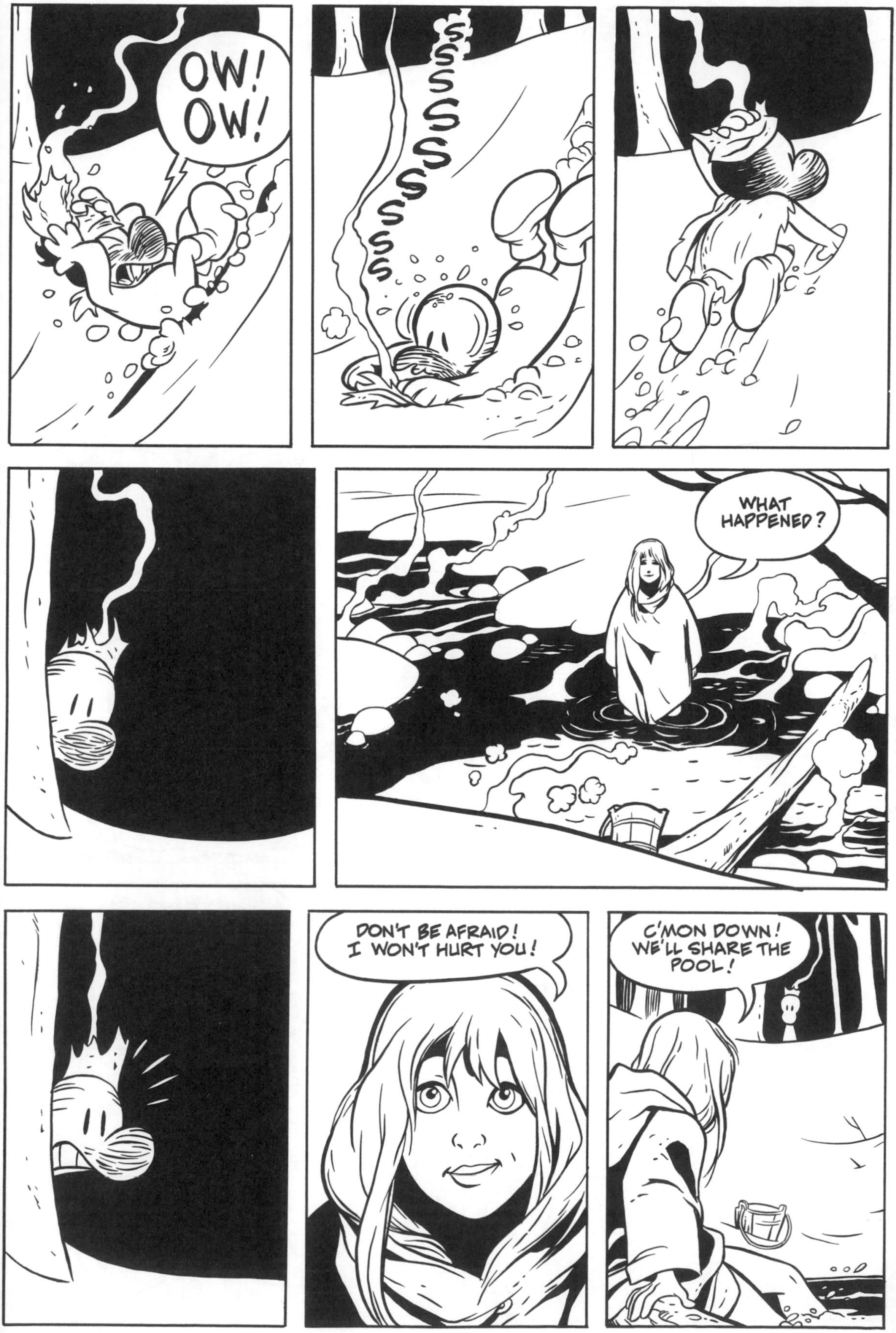
OW! OW!
SSSSSSSSSS
WHAT HAPPENED?
DON'T BE AFRAID! I WON'T HURT YOU!
C'MON DOWN! WE'LL SHARE THE POOL!

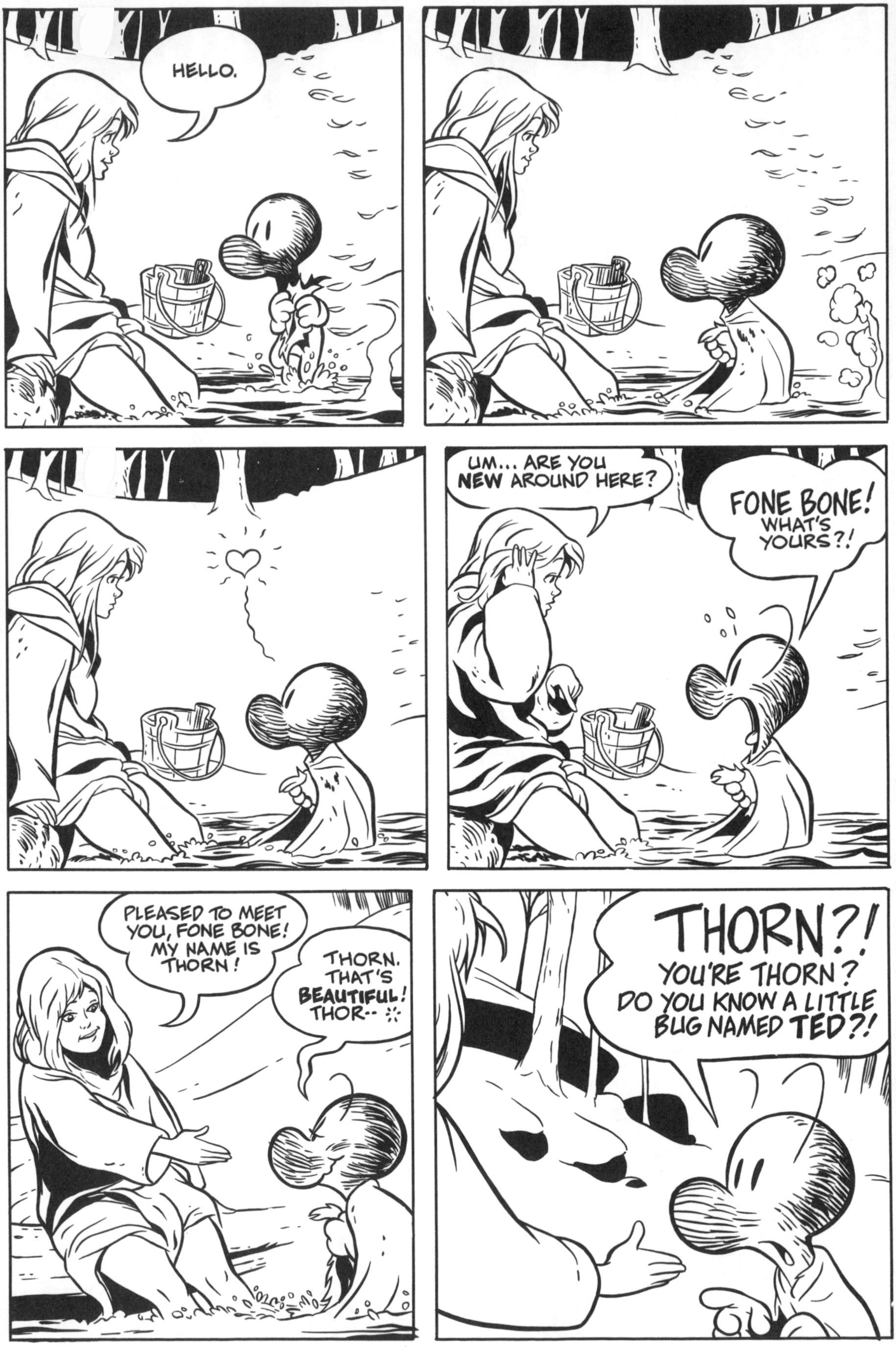
HELLO.
UM... ARE YOU NEW AROUND HERE?
FONE BONE! WHAT'S YOURS?!
PLEASED TO MEET YOU, FONE BONE! MY NAME IS THORN!
THORN. THAT'S BEAUTIFUL! THOR--
THORN?! YOU'RE THORN? DO YOU KNOW A LITTLE BUG NAMED TED?!

51

MY! YOU MUST'VE **ENJOYED** YOUR FIRST NIGHT IN A HOUSE AFTER SLEEPING IN THE **WOODS**! YOU DIDN'T EVEN **HEAR** ME WHEN I CAME DOWNSTAIRS!

CAKES?

HERE'S YOUR CAKES! AND HERE'S SOME TEA!

THENK YOU.

HELLO? ARE YOU **AWAKE** YET, FONE BONE? IT'S **ME**, THORN!

THORN?

HOW ABOUT IF WE GET THE FIREWOOD **LATER**?

SIGH.

SO... DO YOU THINK YOUR GRAN'MA WILL MIND ME **STAYIN'** WITH YOU GUYS? I MEAN-- I DON'T WANNA CAUSE ANY PROBLEMS!

SHE WON'T MIND! SHE WOULDN'T MAKE YOU GO BACK OUT IN THE **WOODS**-- ESPECIALLY WITH THOSE **RAT CREATURES** AROUND!

I HOPE NOT.

JUST DO ME ONE FAVOR! WHEN GRAN'MA BEN GETS HERE, **TRY** NOT TO MENTION YOUR FRIEND THE **DRAGON**!

WHY NOT?

BECAUSE DRAGONS DON'T **EXIST**, THAT'S WHY!

WHAT DO YOU **MEAN**? YOU BELIEVE IN **RAT CREATURES**! WHY DON'T YOU BELIEVE IN **DRAGONS**?

BECAUSE **EVERYBODY** BELIEVES IN RAT CREATURES! BUT **YOU'RE** THE ONLY ONE WHO'S EVER SEEN A **DRAGON**!

I DON'T BELIEVE IT!

62

63

GRUMP!
GRUMP!
GRUMP!

GRUMP!

SPLOP

SPLOOSH

OOOH! WAIT'LL I GET MY HANDS ON THAT COUSIN OF MINE!

I CAN'T **BELIEVE** FONE BONE WOULD JUST **LEAVE** ME OUT HERE WANDERING AROUND HELPLESS AND HUNGRY!

I'LL BET HE'S BACK IN BONEVILLE **RIGHT NOW,** SITTING IN **MY** HOUSE, EATING **MY** FOOD!

GLORP!
RUMBLE!
GRRRR

GROWL!

HEY! **SHUT UP!** I JUST ATE A **STICK** AN HOUR AGO! WHAT DO YOU **WANT** FROM ME?!

70

71

73

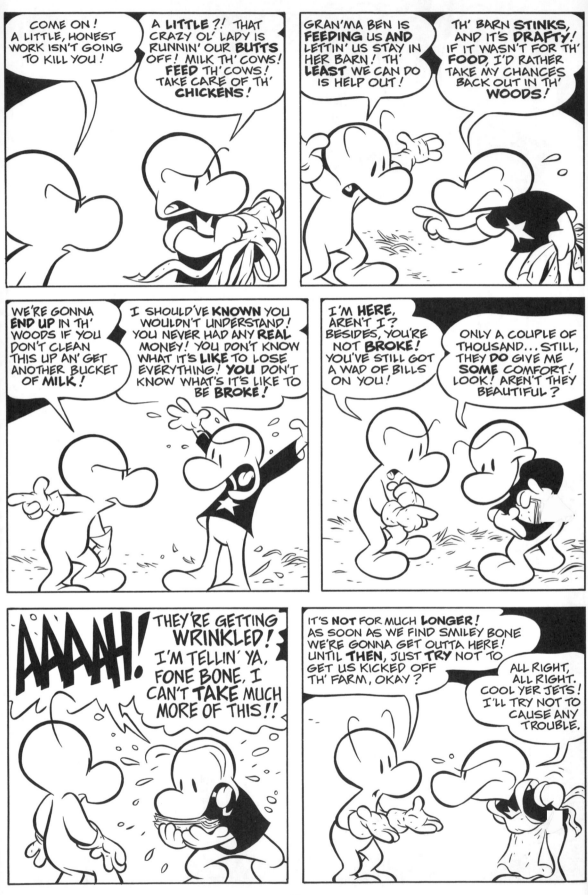

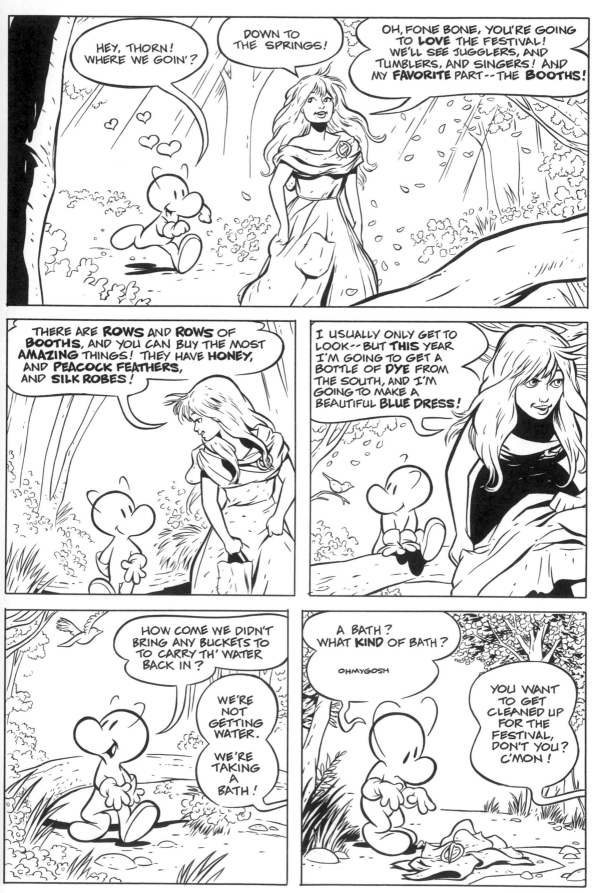

85

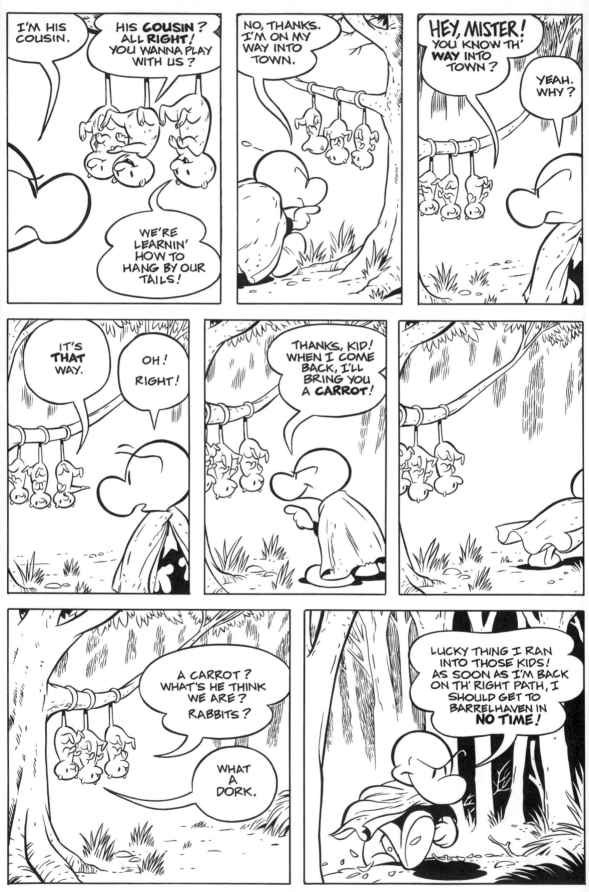

WE TRIED TO SPY.... BUT THE DRAGON TREDS A WIDE CIRCLE AROUND HIM...

THE CREATURE IS ON A SMALL FARM NEAR THE HOT SPRINGS... HE STAYS WITH THE OLD COW WOMAN ...MOTHER BEN.....

...., THESE ARE GRAVE TIDINGS....IT WOULD NOT BE WELL FOR THE DRAGON TO LEARN OF OUR PLANS....

....IF WE MUST RISK A CONFRONTATION..... WE MUST DO IT NOW... WHILE THE DRAGON'S SUSPICIONS SLEEP....

KINGDOK...PREPARE TWO WAR PARTIES....TAKE A THOUSAND WARRIORS IN EACH....

WITH THE FIRST.... SCOUR THE COUNTRYSIDE.. SEARCH THE ROAD AND THE LANDS BEYOND THE WATERFALL.... FIND THE ONE WHO BEARS THE STAR.....

....IF THE DRAGON IS STILL WATCHING....THIS ACTIVITY WILL DRAW HIM OFF...LEAVING THE OLD COW WOMAN UNGUARDED.....

SEND THE SECOND PARTY TO THE FARM HOUSE..... ... DESTROY IT....... ...KILL THE NEW CREATURE...

LET US HOPE THAT THE DEATH OF THIS FONE BONE WILL CAUSE THE DRAGON TO LEAVE THE VALLEY AND RETURN TO DEREN GARD....

...GO NOW.... WE ATTACK TONIGHT

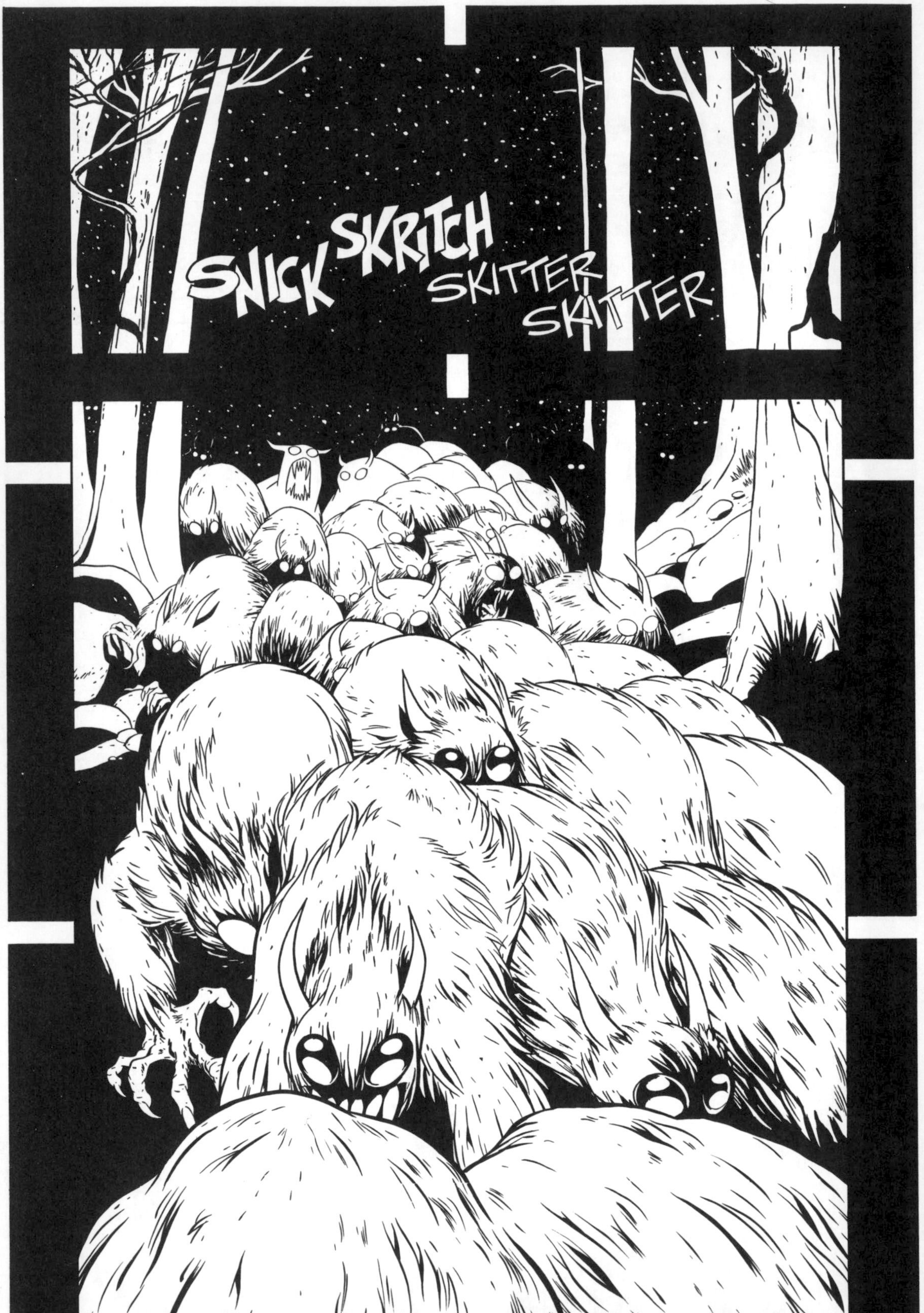
SNICK SKRITCH
SKITTER
SKITTER

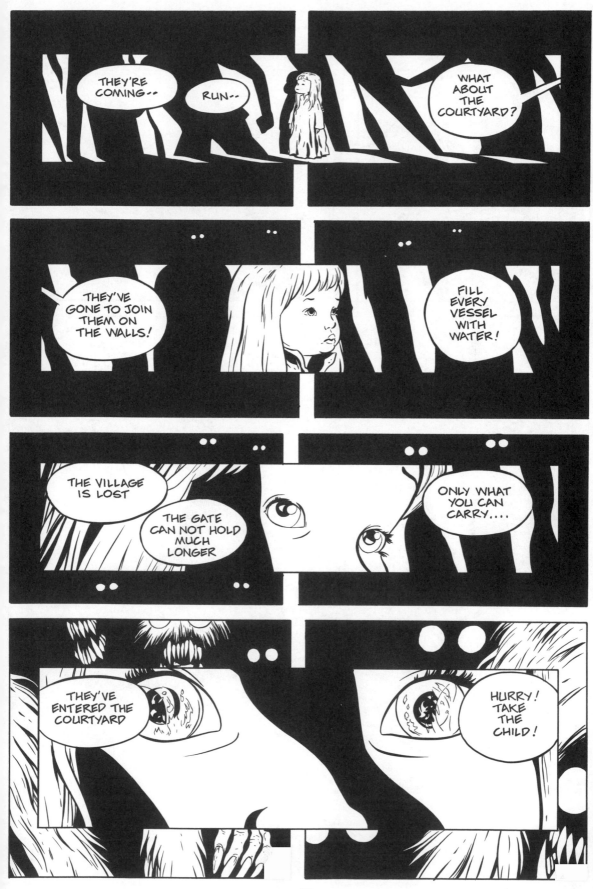

BONE

GRAN'MA?! WHAT'S GOING ON?!

WHERE ARE THEY?

THEY'VE SURROUNDED THE HOUSE.... HURRY DOWN HERE!

DO YOU THINK IT'S SAFE TO HAVE ALL THESE **LIGHTS** BURNIN'? MAYBE WE SHOULD **DOUSE** 'EM!

NO. TH' LIGHTS ARE KEEPIN' TH' MONSTERS **BACK**!

IF IT WAS **DARK** IN HERE, AN' THE RAT CREATURES THOUGHT WE WERE **ASLEEP** -- WE'D BE **DEAD** RIGHT NOW.

GET UP! GET UP!

103

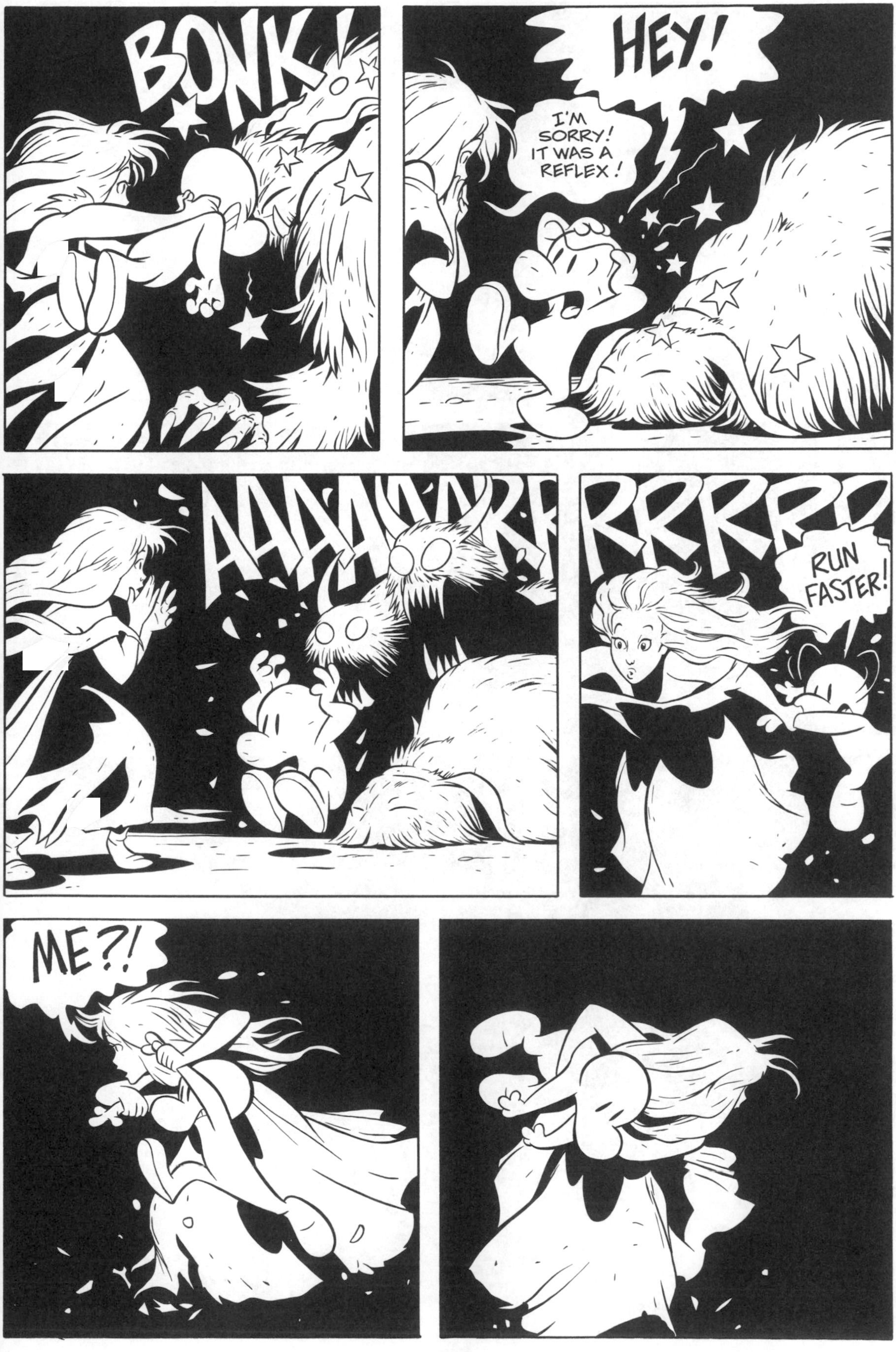
BONK!
HEY!
I'M SORRY! IT WAS A REFLEX!
AAAAAARRRRRRRR
RUN FASTER!
ME?!

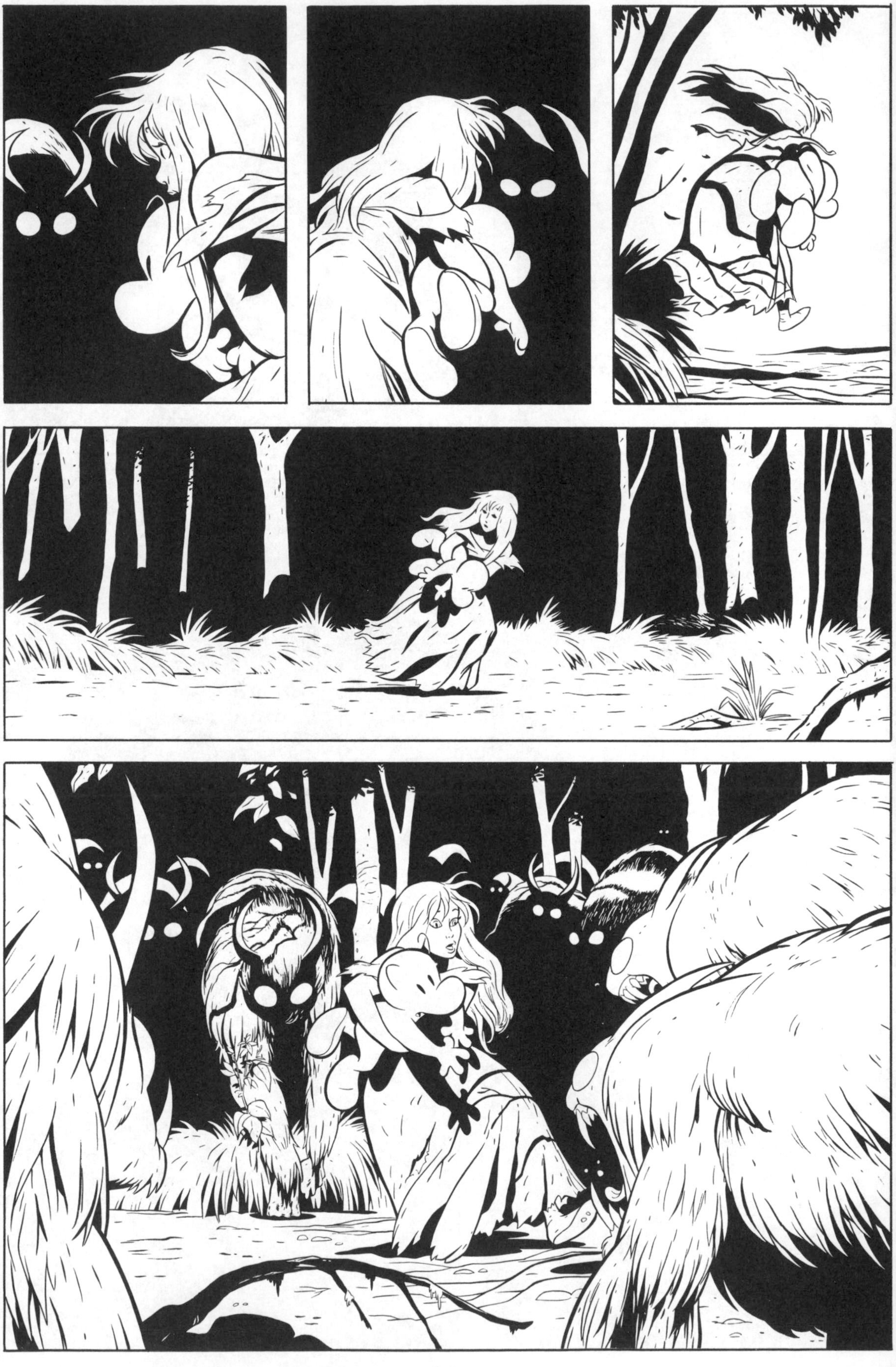

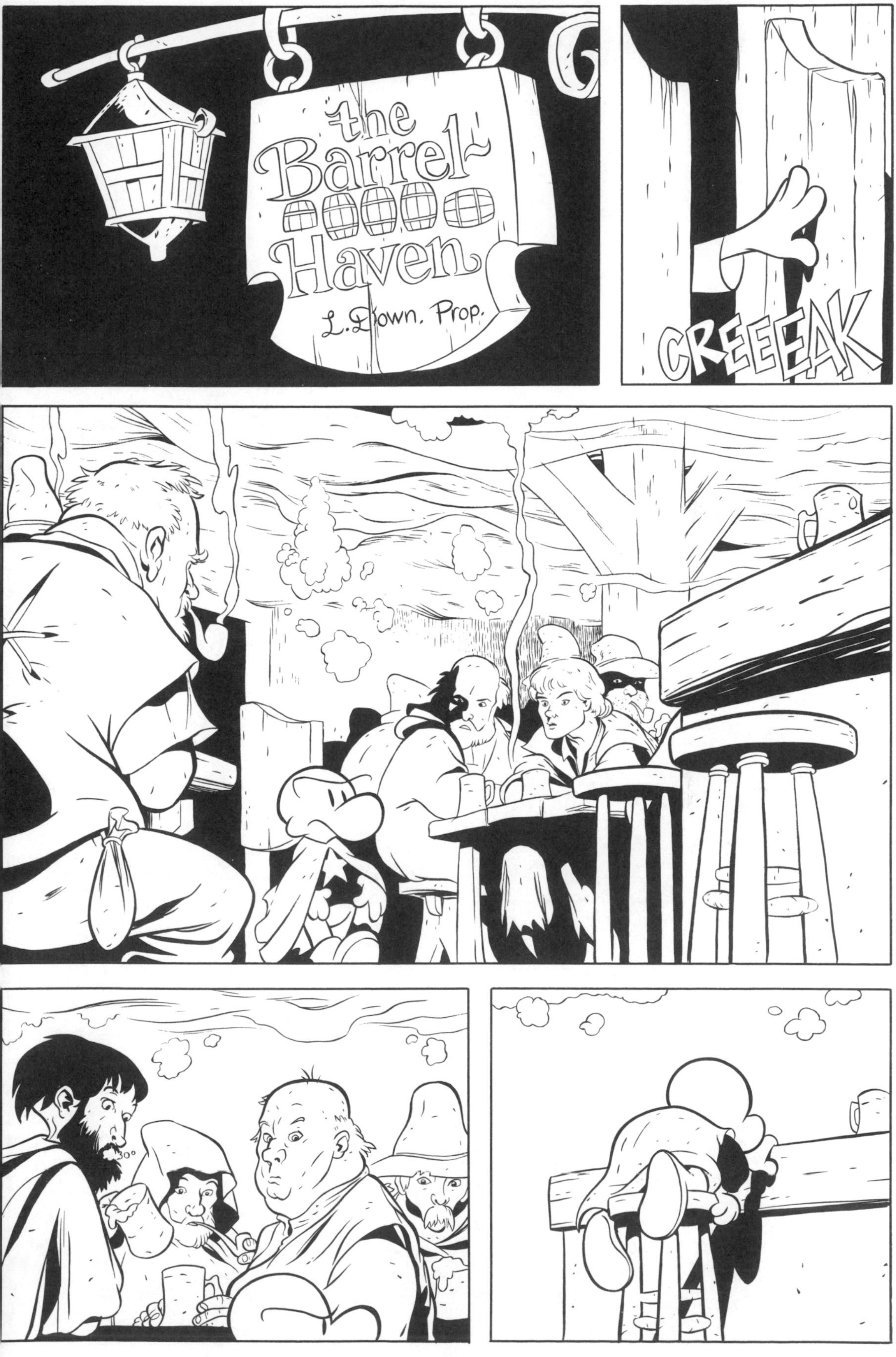
the Barrel Haven
L. Down. Prop.
CREEEAK

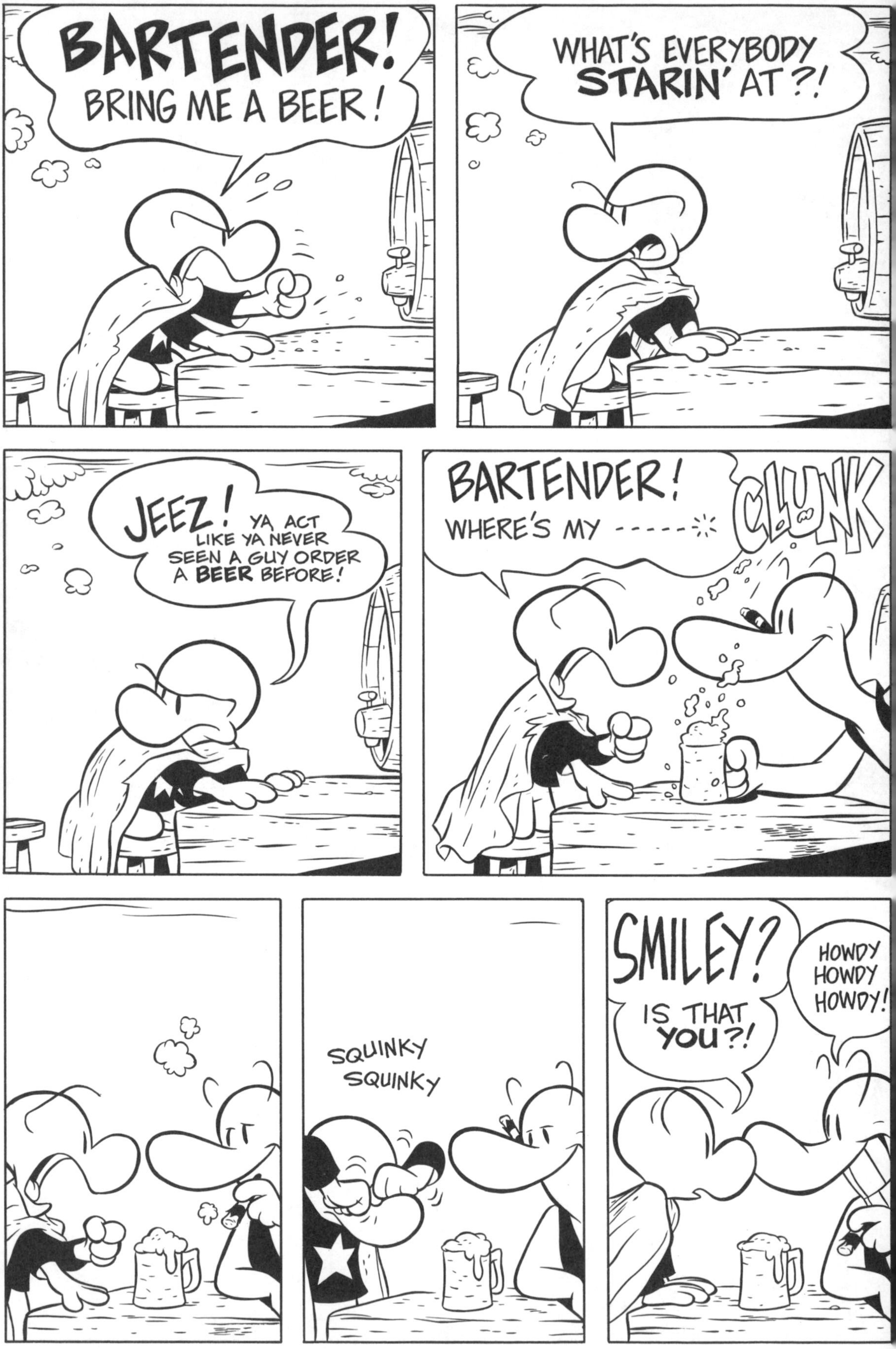
BARTENDER! BRING ME A BEER!
WHAT'S EVERYBODY STARIN' AT?!
JEEZ! YA ACT LIKE YA NEVER SEEN A GUY ORDER A BEER BEFORE!
BARTENDER! WHERE'S MY -----
CLUNK
SQUINKY SQUINKY
SMILEY? IS THAT YOU?!
HOWDY HOWDY HOWDY!

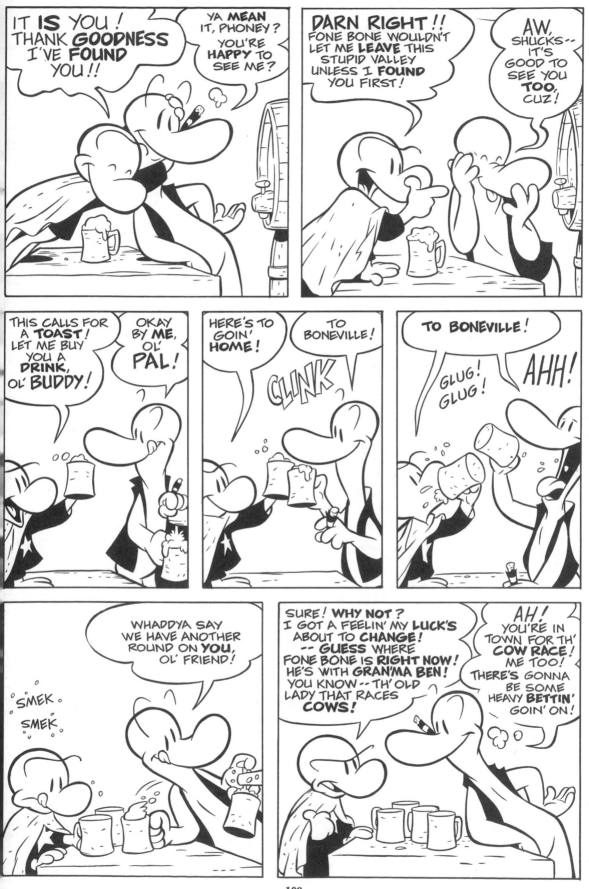

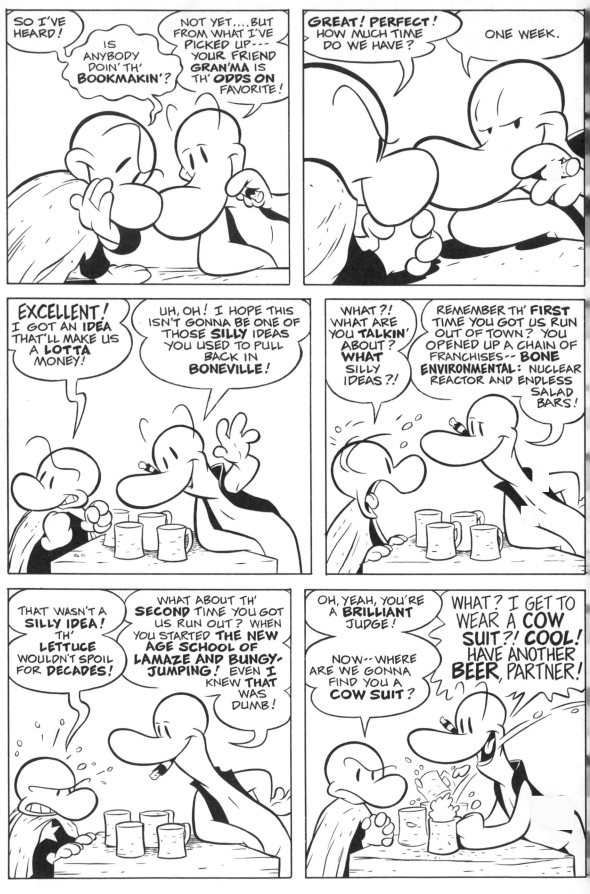

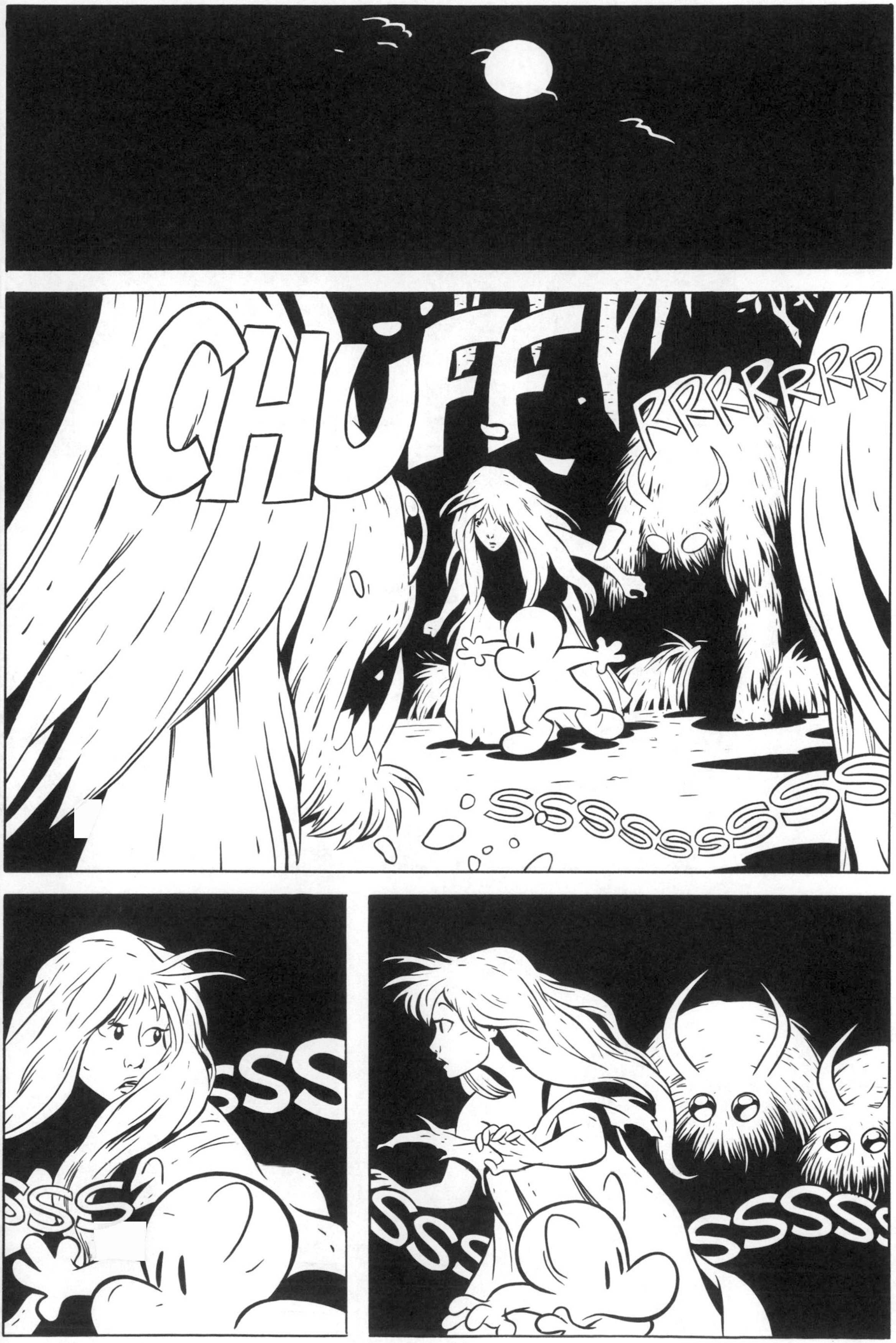
CHUFF
RRRRRRRR
SSSSSSSSSS
SSS
SSS
SSS
SSSSS

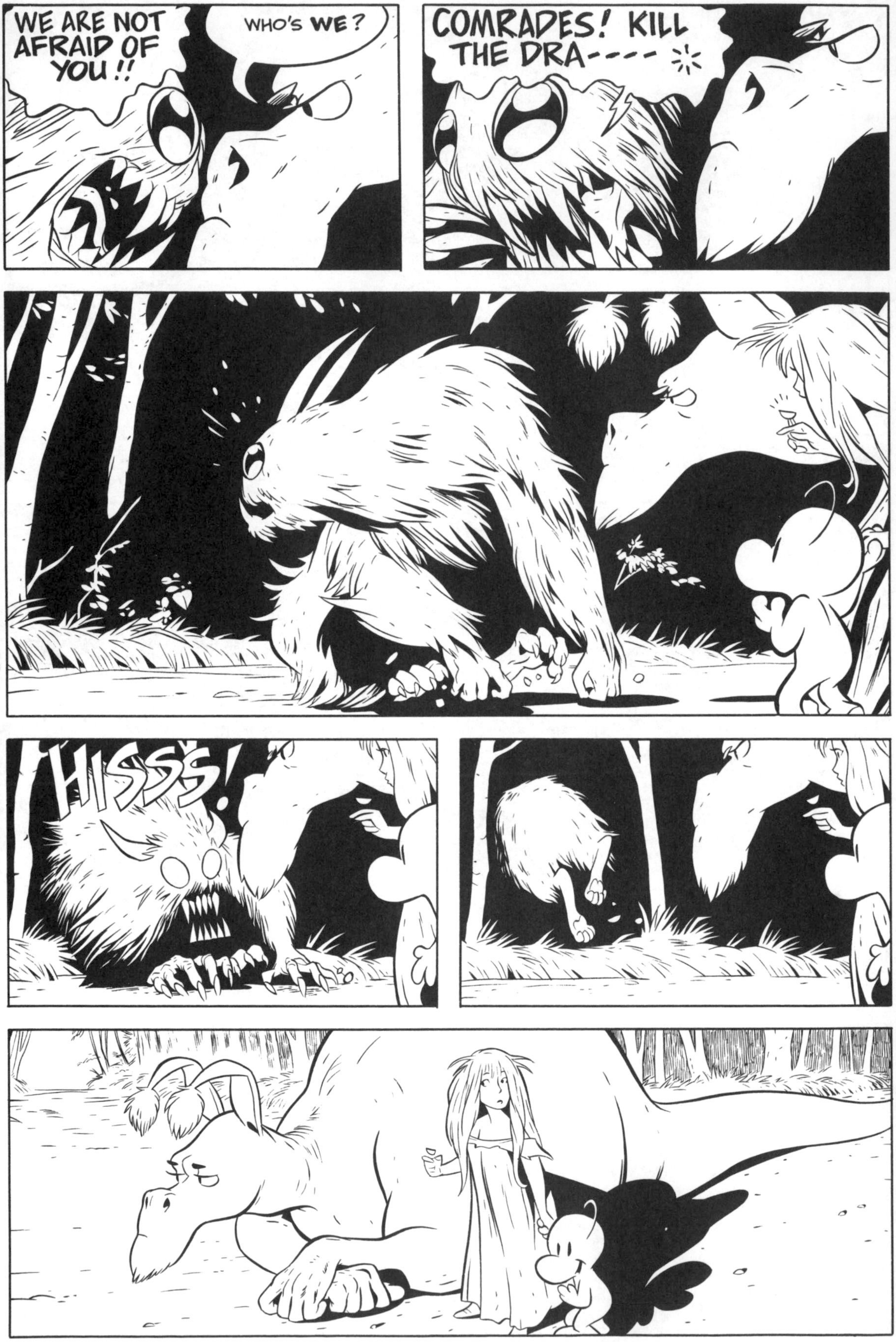
WE ARE NOT AFRAID OF YOU!!
WHO'S WE?
COMRADES! KILL THE DRA----
HISSS!

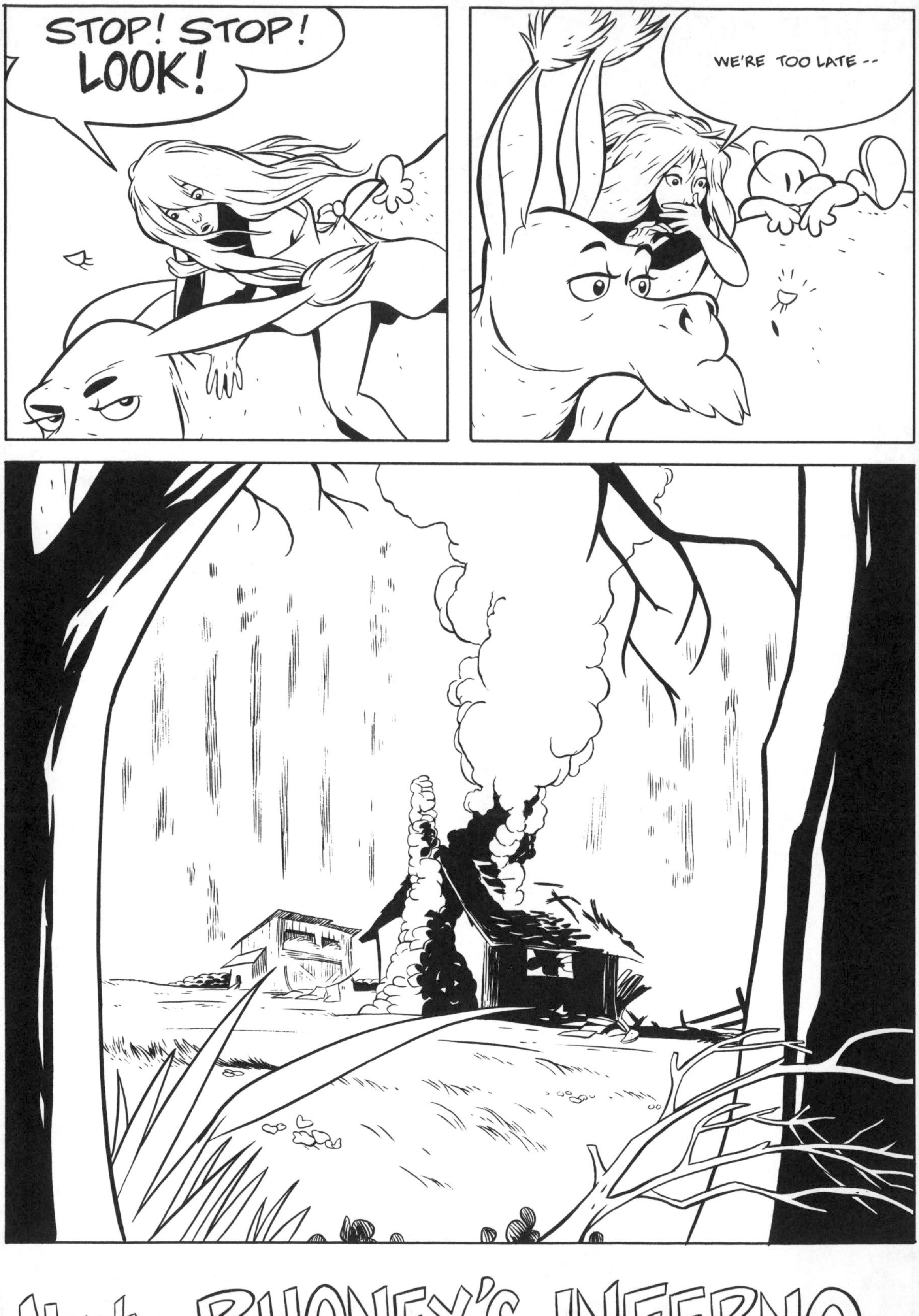
STOP! STOP! LOOK!
WE'RE TOO LATE --

Next: PHONEY'S INFERNO

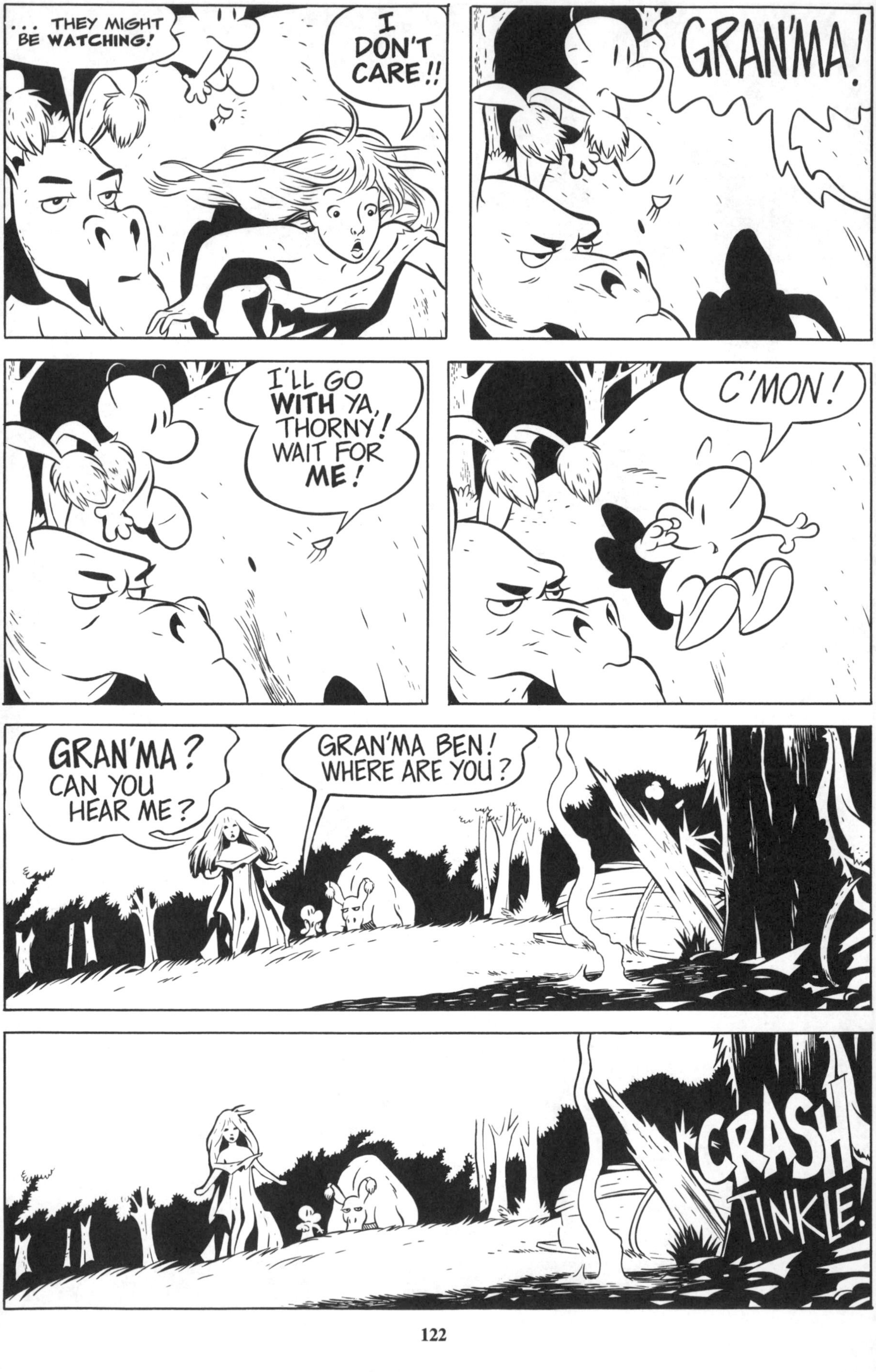

... THEY MIGHT BE WATCHING!
I DON'T CARE!!
GRAN'MA!
I'LL GO WITH YA, THORNY! WAIT FOR ME!
C'MON!
GRAN'MA? CAN YOU HEAR ME?
GRAN'MA BEN! WHERE ARE YOU?
CRASH!
TINKLE!

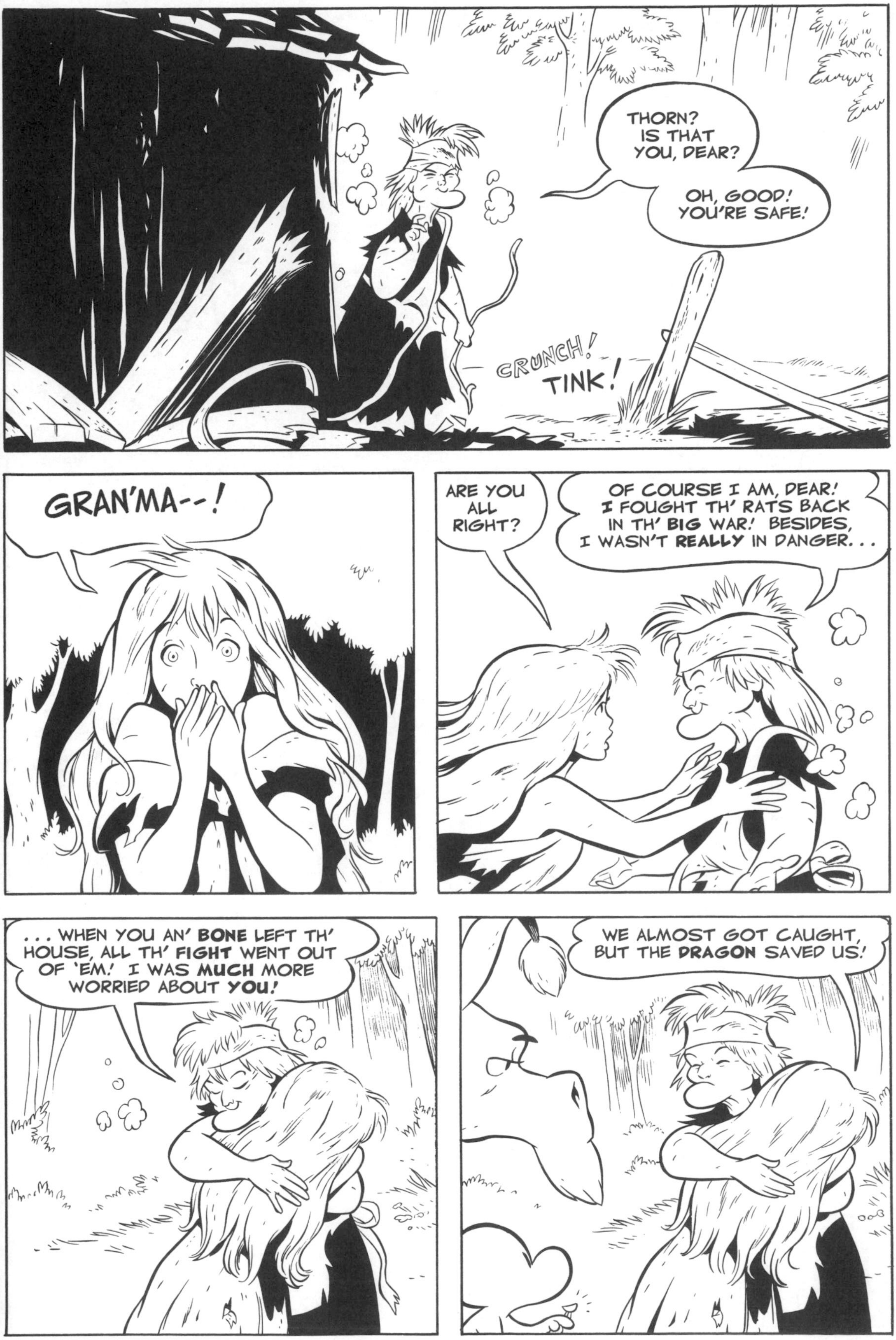
THORN? IS THAT YOU, DEAR?
OH, GOOD! YOU'RE SAFE!
CRUNCH!
TINK!
GRAN'MA--!
ARE YOU ALL RIGHT?
OF COURSE I AM, DEAR! I FOUGHT TH' RATS BACK IN TH' BIG WAR! BESIDES, I WASN'T REALLY IN DANGER...
...WHEN YOU AN' BONE LEFT TH' HOUSE, ALL TH' FIGHT WENT OUT OF 'EM! I WAS MUCH MORE WORRIED ABOUT YOU!
WE ALMOST GOT CAUGHT, BUT THE DRAGON SAVED US!

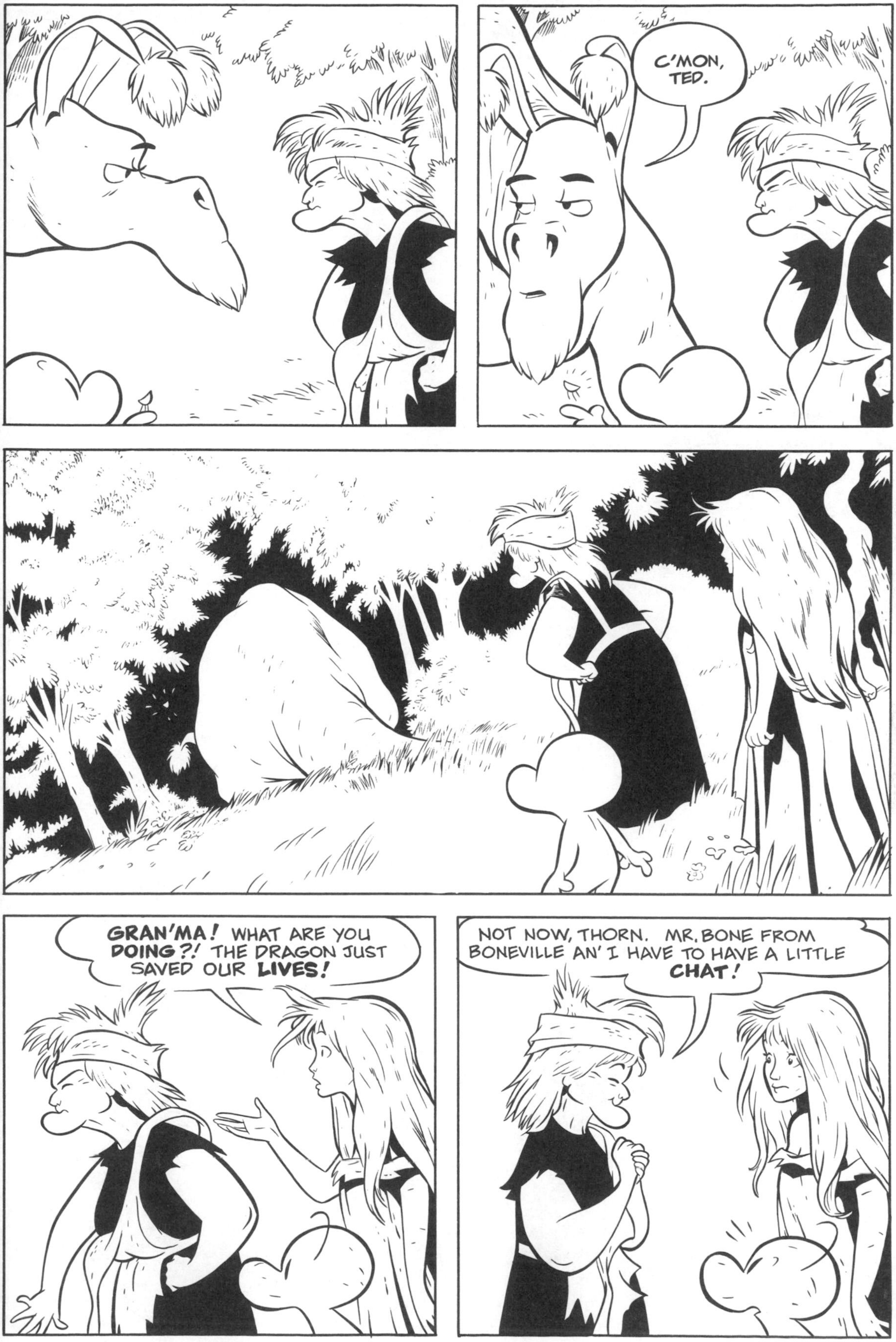
C'MON, TED.
GRAN'MA! WHAT ARE YOU DOING?! THE DRAGON JUST SAVED OUR LIVES!
NOT NOW, THORN. MR. BONE FROM BONEVILLE AN' I HAVE TO HAVE A LITTLE CHAT!

127

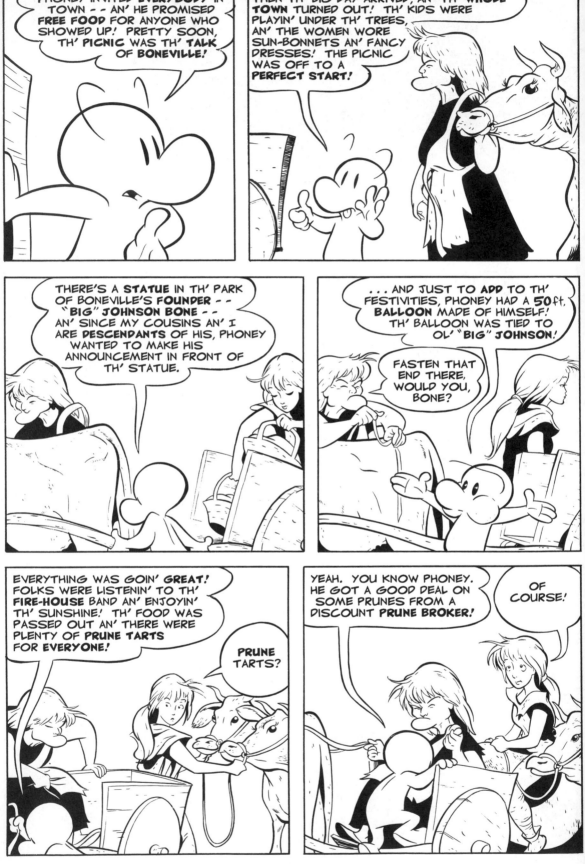

PHONEY INVITED **EVERYBODY** IN TOWN -- AN' HE PROMISED **FREE FOOD** FOR ANYONE WHO SHOWED UP! PRETTY SOON, TH' **PICNIC** WAS TH' **TALK** OF **BONEVILLE!**

THEN TH' **BIG** DAY ARRIVED, AN' TH' **WHOLE TOWN** TURNED OUT! TH' KIDS WERE PLAYIN' UNDER TH' TREES, AN' THE WOMEN WORE SUN-BONNETS AN' FANCY DRESSES! THE PICNIC WAS OFF TO A **PERFECT START!**

THERE'S A **STATUE** IN TH' PARK OF BONEVILLE'S **FOUNDER** -- "BIG" JOHNSON BONE -- AN' SINCE MY COUSINS AN' I ARE **DESCENDANTS** OF HIS, PHONEY WANTED TO MAKE HIS ANNOUNCEMENT IN FRONT OF TH' STATUE.

... AND JUST TO **ADD** TO TH' FESTIVITIES, PHONEY HAD A **50**ft. **BALLOON** MADE OF HIMSELF! TH' BALLOON WAS TIED TO OL' "BIG" **JOHNSON!**

FASTEN THAT END THERE, WOULD YOU, BONE?

EVERYTHING WAS GOIN' **GREAT!** FOLKS WERE LISTENIN' TO TH' **FIRE-HOUSE** BAND AN' ENJOYIN' TH' SUNSHINE! TH' FOOD WAS PASSED OUT AN' THERE WERE PLENTY OF **PRUNE TARTS** FOR **EVERYONE!**

PRUNE TARTS?

YEAH. YOU KNOW PHONEY. HE GOT A GOOD DEAL ON SOME PRUNES FROM A DISCOUNT **PRUNE BROKER!**

OF COURSE!

128

HEY, SMILEY! TAKE THAT TUB OF GLASSES BACK TO YOUR BUDDY! WE'RE OUT OF MUGS AGAIN!

YES, SIR, MISTER DOWN!

HEY, THERE, PHONEY! LUCIUS SAYS YA GOTTA WASH THESE, PRONTO! WE GOT A LOT OF THIRSTY CUSTOMERS OUT FRONT!

OF COURSE, I MAKE SURE EVERYBODY GETS A NEW, CLEAN MUG WITH EACH DRINK!

YEAH. I NOTICED.

CLUNK

... I JUST WANT YOU TO KNOW ... I'VE BEEN **WORKING** ON **THE PLAN!** I BEEN SPREADIN' **RUMORS** ALL DAY THAT **GRAN'MA BEN** IS **TOO OLD** TO WIN TH' RACE THIS YEAR!

IS ANYBODY **BUYIN'** IT?

I'M TH' **BARTENDER!** THEY **GOTTA** BELIEVE ME!

THIS IS **TOO** EASY! WE'LL COVER ALL TH' **BETS,** AND THEN WHEN GRAN'MA **WINS,** WE'LL BE **RICH!**

OF COURSE, WHEN GRAN'MA GETS INTO **TOWN,** EVERYBODY'S GONNA **SEE** SHE'S PERFECTLY **FIT!**

I'VE GOT THAT COVERED WITH PHASE **TWO:** **THE MYSTERY COW!** A **COW** THAT WE'LL **BUILD UP** IN EVERYBODY'S IMAGINATION THAT **CAN'T** BE BEAT!

WAIT! IS **THAT** TH' PART WHERE I GET TO WEAR TH' **COW SUIT?!** OH, **JOY!**

YEAH, **THAT'S** TH' PART! BUT YOU'RE GONNA **THROW** TH' RACE! REMEMBER! WE **WANT** GRAN'MA BEN TO **WIN!**

WELL, **NATURALLY,** I'M LOOKING FORWARD TO WEARIN' A **COW SUIT** -- BUT WHAT DO **YOU** GET OUT OF IT? AFTER **ALL,** THE LOCALS DON'T USE **MONEY!** THEY TRADE **GOODS 'N' SERVICES!**

IT **DOES** SOUR MY PLANS FOR AMASSING A **HUGE** FORTUNE AND RETURNING TO BONEVILLE IN **TRIUMPH** ... STILL, THE PLAY IS TH' THING!

IF ALL THESE YOKELS HAVE ARE **POULTRY PRODUCTS,** THEN I'LL **TAKE IT!!**

131

133

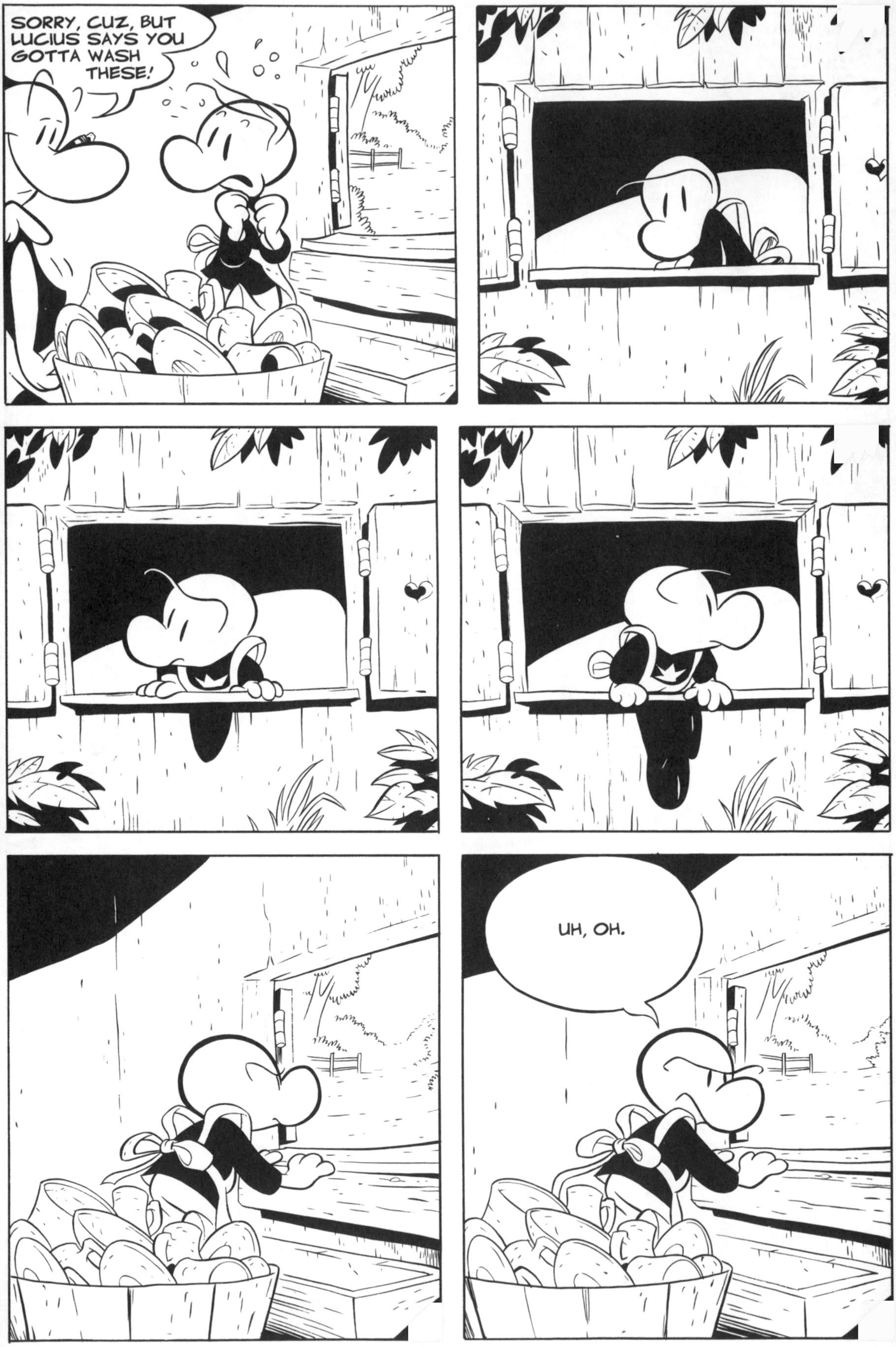
SORRY, CUZ, BUT LUCIUS SAYS YOU GOTTA WASH THESE!
UH, OH.

135

136

WELL, WELL . . . IT'S ABOUT **TIME**!

HELLO, LUCIUS!

HOW YA DOIN', ROSIE? WAS TH' **ROAD** SAFE? I WAS **WORRIED** ABOUT YA!

TH' **ROAD** WAS CLEAR . . . EXCEPT FOR YOUR **ROADBLOCK**!

OH! I GOT SOMETHIN' FOR YA! **HERE**! I BEEN SAVIN' IT IN MY POCKET ALL DAY!

OH, AREN'T YOU SWEET!

. . . WELLL . . . . . I HAD A LITTLE EXTRA **TIME** ON MY HANDS THIS MORNING . . .

. . . I GOT A COUPLE OF **DEAD BEATS** INSIDE TAKIN' CARE OF TH' **CUSTOMERS** — IN FACT, THEY LOOK A **LOT** LIKE THIS LITTLE FELLA YOU GOT HERE.

THEY **DO**?!

139

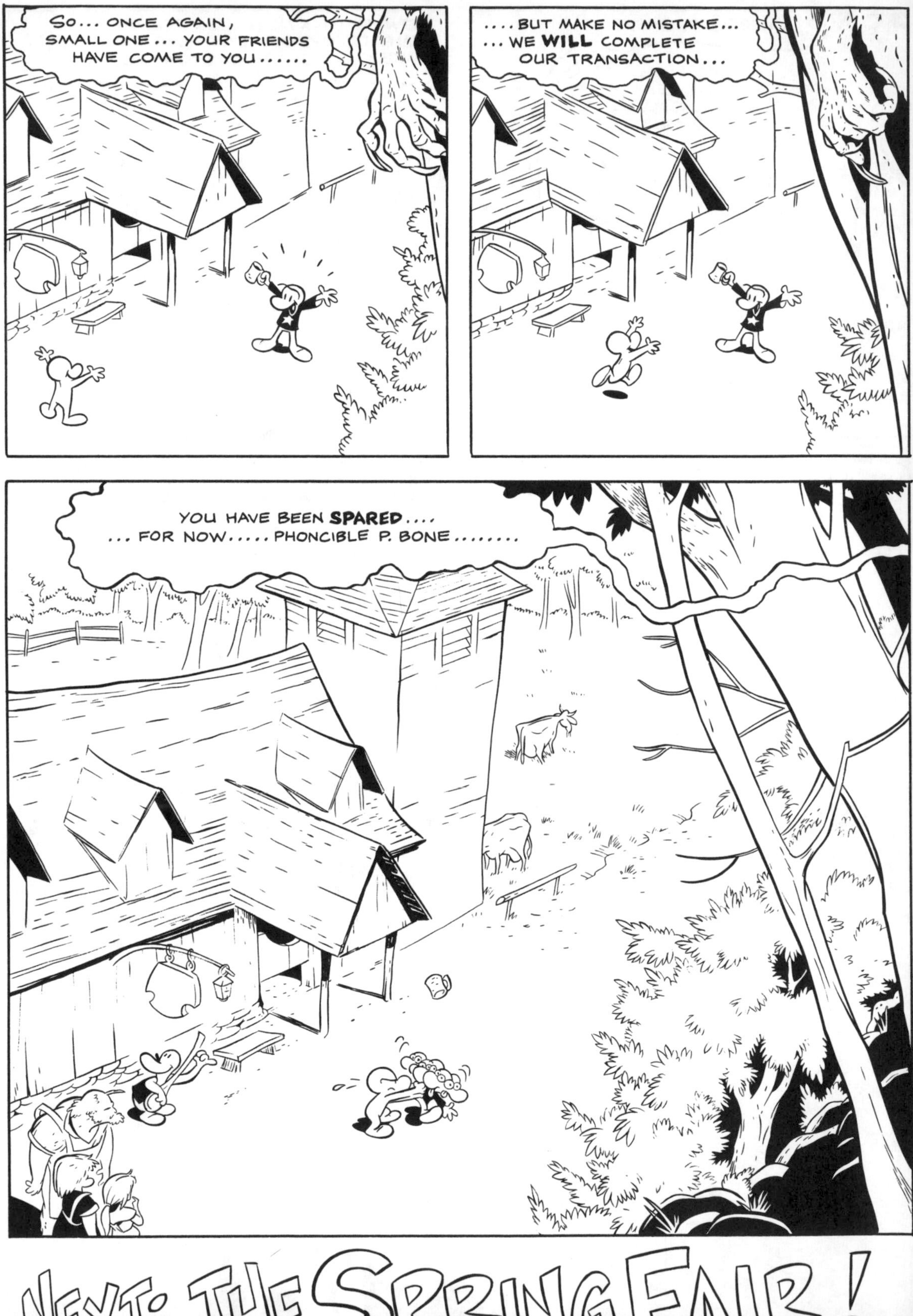

SO... ONCE AGAIN, SMALL ONE... YOUR FRIENDS HAVE COME TO YOU......
....BUT MAKE NO MISTAKE... ...WE **WILL** COMPLETE OUR TRANSACTION...
YOU HAVE BEEN **SPARED**.... ...FOR NOW.....PHONCIBLE P. BONE........
NEXT: THE SPRING FAIR!

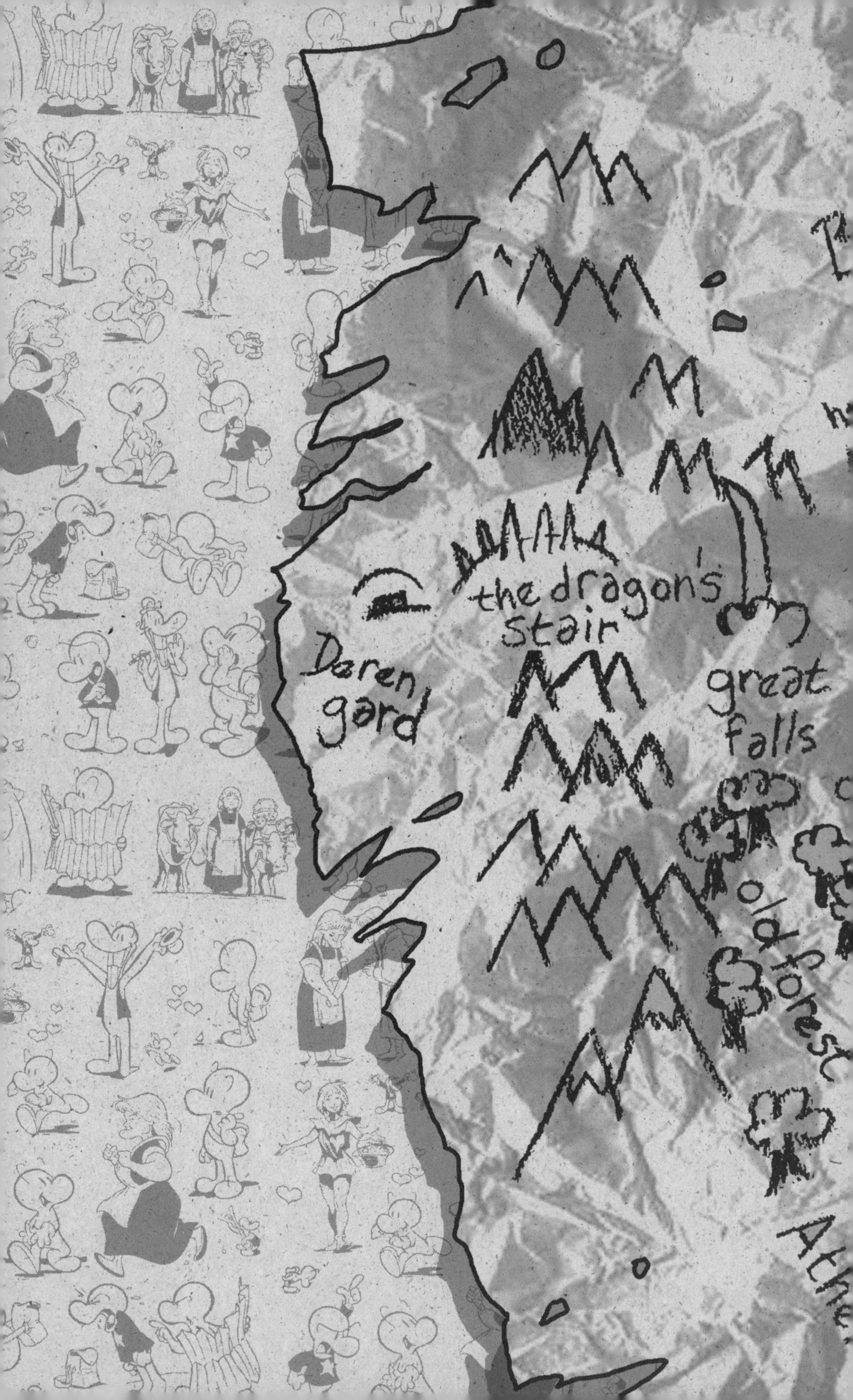
the dragon's stair
Daren gard
great falls
old forest